E. L. Konigsburg

Twayne's United States Authors Series
Children's Literature

Ruth K. MacDonald, Editor
Purdue University Calumet

TUSAS 608

E. L. Konigsburg. Photograph by Bill Sykes/*Florida Times-Union*

E. L. Konigsburg

Dorrel Thomas Hanks, Jr.
Baylor University

Twayne Publishers • New York

Maxwell Macmillan Canada • *Toronto*

Maxwell Macmillan International • *New York Oxford Singapore Sydney*

Twayne Publishers
Macmillan Publishing Company
866 Third Avenue
New York, New York 10022

Maxwell Macmillan Canada, Inc.
1200 Eglinton Avenue East
Suite 200
Don Mills, Ontario M3C 3N1

Macmillan Publishing Company is a part of the Maxwell Communication Group of Companies.

Library of Congress Cataloging-in-Publication Data

Hanks, Dorrel Thomas.
    E. L. Konigsburg / by Dorrel Thomas. Hanks, Jr.
        p. cm. — (Twayne's United States authors series.
Children's literature)
    Includes bibliographical references and index.
    ISBN 0-8057-3970-X (alk. paper)
    1. Konigsburg, E. L.—Criticism and interpretation. 2.
Children's stories, American—History and criticism. I. Title. II.
Series.
PS3561.0459Z6 1992
813'.54—dc20   92-302
                                                            CIP

The paper used in this publication meets the minimum requirements of American National Standard for Information Sciences—Permanence of Paper for Printed Library Materials, ANSI Z39.48-1984.

10 9 8 7 6 5 4 3 2 1

Printed in the United States of America.

To Carole, Kirsten, and Thomas,
who have illuminated
Konigsburg's books for me

Contents

Preface

In 1968, for the first and (so far) only time since the Newbery Award and the Newbery Honor Award were instituted in 1922, one author won both awards for the best and the second best children's book published in the previous year. That author was Elaine Lobl Konigsburg, a suburban housewife who had never written a novel before. Winning both awards in the same year is the equivalent of training the horses that finish first and second in the Kentucky Derby; the double triumph definitely promised that E. L. Konigsburg would become a major author of children's literature.[1]

She has fulfilled that promise, writing 12 more books and several essays since 1968. In those 22 years, however, only three critics have studied her works at length: Eric Kimmel, David Rees, and John Rowe Townsend. Kimmel addresses only a single work, *About the B'nai Bagels*; Rees discusses several of the early works, but only briefly; and Townsend deals with Konigsburg's oeuvre as of 1978, but is restricted to a 12-page essay.[2]

The time has come for a full-length study of all Konigsburg's works as of 1992—first, because she is a Newbery winner and has written 14 still-in-print books translated into eight languages,[3] and, second and possibly more important, because of the theme of identity she pursues in all but her recent picture books—a theme of great importance to her 8- to 14-year-old audience. As she put it in her Newbery Award acceptance speech in 1968, she includes a dual topic in each book: American suburbia and a child's search for identity there.

Konigsburg encapsulated her thematic concern in a 1986 interview: "Each author really has *a* theme, and Identity apparently is mine."[4] About her choice to write for the "middle-aged" child of 10 to 14, she added, "It is the age at which the pull of the peer group is so strong a child can lose his sense of self," explaining that this is the very age at which a child must establish his/her sense of self.[5] Child psychologist Erik Erikson would agree: in his classic *Identity: Youth and Crisis* he says that the development of individual identity is a chief task of the 8 to 14 year old—a task that must be accomplished if the child is to mature.[6]

Konigsburg shows this "task" to her child readers from a perspective that allows them to distance themselves from their own identity struggles and thus to see those struggles in a new light. Arguments with siblings, anger at parents who "do not understand," coping with divorce and a single parent—these can be grim elements of a child's life. Konigsburg handles these and other developmental themes lightly; her consistent wit removes some of their weight and helps child readers gain perspective on their own development.

Both the theme of identity and a suburban setting appear in virtually all of Konigsburg's fiction (i.e., the nonhistorical, non-picture-book works). Given the same theme, and roughly the same setting, for each novel, it might appear that Konigsburg is writing formula fiction, doing hack work. She is not. Despite the presence of these two interrelated elements in most of her books, each book is unique.

They are unique first with respect to their plots. For example, who would ever think of two children running away from home to New York's Metropolitan Museum of Art—there to take up residence until they decide to return home? That plan is the center of *From the Mixed-up Files of Mrs. Basil E. Frankweiler.* Second, they are unique in terms of characterization and Konigsburg's witty style. Indeed, it is chiefly her wit, as I suggest later in the text, that distinguishes Konigsburg's work from that of other top-rank writers for children. Her illustrations, too, deserve special note. Aside from such author-artists as Maurice Sendak and Tomi de Paola who write for the very young, few children's authors illustrate their own books. Almost no children's novelists do so. Konigsburg does. Removing the illustrator who normally stands between author and audience, Konigsburg provides through her illustrations exactly what she wants her readers to see of setting and characterization, sometimes even of theme. The illustrations enrich their texts.

A discussion of those elements, then—plot and setting, characterization, style (and/or technique), theme, and the contribution of Konigsburg's illustrations—comprises most of this study. I discuss the works in roughly chronological order, but considerations of genre have assured the historical novels and the two books of short stories chapters of their own. Throughout the text I have, where appropriate, compared Konigsburg's novels to those of other writers.

Acknowledgments

I must first thank Elaine Lobl Konigsburg for her friendly willingness to grant me interviews in person and by telephone. "Time is finite," she once told me; I greatly appreciate her sharing some of her time with me.

I also appreciate Baylor University's supporting this study by granting me a series of released-time fellowships for writing and financial support for travel to interview Mrs. Konigsburg. I am likewise grateful to the personnel of Baylor's Moody Memorial Library for their constant support and professionalism. I note my colleague Ginger Thornton. Her keen editing has made this a better book. Barbara Sutton of Twayne Publishers has likewise improved the book. I am grateful to both.

Permission to use illustrations from E. L. Konigsburg's published works has been granted by Atheneum Publishers, an imprint of Macmillan Publishing Co. Permission to quote from her unpublished essays has been granted by Mrs. Konigsburg herself. The *Florida Times-Union* granted permission to use its photograph of Mrs. Konigsburg for the cover and frontispiece.

Finally, I should note that my research into recent children's literature other than Konigsburg's has been greatly aided by two books: Bernice E. Cullinan's *Literature and the Child*, 2d ed. (New York: Harcourt Brace Jovanovich, 1989), and Betsy Hearne's *Choosing Books for Children*, rev. ed. (New York: Delacorte, 1990).

Chronology

1930	Elaine Lobl born 10 February in New York City to Adolph and Beulah Lobl; family moves to Phoenixville, Pennsylvania.
1939	Family moves to Youngstown, Ohio.
1941	Family moves to Farrell, Pennsylvania.
1947	Graduates from Farrell High School, highest honors.
1947–1948	Keeps books for Shenango Valley Provision Company, Sharon, Pennsylvania. Meets David Konigsburg.
1952	Graduates from Carnegie Mellon Institute of Technology (now Carnegie Mellon University) with a B.S. in chemistry. Marries David Konigsburg.
1952–1954	Does graduate work in chemistry at the University of Pittsburgh.
1954	Moves to Jacksonville, Florida.
1954–1955	Teaches science in Bartram School (a private girls' school), Jacksonville, Florida.
1955	Son, Paul, born. Temporarily leaves Bartram School.
1956	Daughter, Laurie, born.
1959	Second son, Ross, born. Begins formal painting lessons at Jacksonville [Florida] Art Museum. Painting wins first prize in Jacksonville County Fair art competition.
1960–1962	Returns to teaching science in Bartram School.

1962–1963   Moves to Saddle Brook, New Jersey. Joins Art Students' League, New York City.

1962–1964   Takes courses at Art Students' League.

1963   Moves to Port Chester, New York (a suburb of New York City).

1965   Begins writing and illustrating *Jennifer, Hecate, Macbeth, William McKinley, and Me, Elizabeth.*

1966   Submits *Jennifer* to Atheneum Press. Begins work on *From the Mixed-up Files of Mrs. Basil E. Frankweiler.*

1967   Submits *Files* to Atheneum Press; moves back to Jacksonville, Florida. *Jennifer* and *Files* published.

1968   Wins Newbery Award for *Files,* Newbery Honor Book Award for *Jennifer.*

1969   *About the B'nai Bagels* published.

1970   Wins the William Allen White Children's Book Award for *Files. (George)* published.

1971   Receives the Carnegie-Mellon Merit Award. *Altogether, One at a Time* (story collection) published.

1973   *A Proud Taste for Scarlet and Miniver* published. The film *The Hideaways* made of *Files.*

1974   *The Dragon in the Ghetto Caper* published. *Proud Taste* named an American Library Association Notable Children's Book.

1975   *The Second Mrs. Giaconda* published; it receives the American Library Association Best Book for Young Adults award.

1976   *Father's Arcane Daughter* published; it receives the American Library Association Best Book for Young Adults award.

1977   *Daughter* named an American Library Association Notable Book for Young Adults.

1979   *Throwing Shadows* (story collection) published.

1980   *Throwing Shadows* named an American Library Association Notable Children's Book.

1982   *Journey to an 800 Number* published.

1986   *Up from Jericho Tel* published.

1987   *Jericho Tel* named an American Library Association Notable Children's Book.

1988   Sells television rights for *Father's Arcane Daughter* to Hallmark Hall of Fame. Begins work on picture book, *Samuel Todd's Book of Great Colors* (originally a private gift for grandson Samuel Todd Konigsburg, then solicited for publication by Atheneum Press).

1989   Commissioned to write entry on Barbara McClintock for *Nobel Prize Annual: 1988*. Begins work on *Samuel Todd's Book of Great Inventions* (picture book).

1990   *Father's Arcane Daughter,* retitled *Caroline?,* appears on Hallmark Hall of Fame. *Samuel Todd's Book of Great Colors* published. *Samuel Todd's Book of Great Inventions* submitted to Atheneum Press.

1991   *Samuel Todd's Book of Great Inventions* published. Begins work on *Amy Elizabeth Explores Bloomingdale's* (picture book).

1992   *Amy Elizabeth Explores Bloomingdale's* in press.

1

Biographical Sketch

Elaine Lobl Konigsburg gave no evidence of wanting to be an author until she became one. One would have thought her far more likely to become a chemist—or, at the furthest stretch, a sketch artist or painter. After all, in her youth she had studied drawing and painting, which led to formal art lessons after her daughter was born; her college training, moreover, was in chemistry. She had never written much, however—a feature story or so and some news stories for the high school paper she co-edited.

She wrote little, in fact, until 1965, when she began writing and illustrating her first book, *Jennifer, Hecate, Macbeth, William McKinley, and Me, Elizabeth*, which won the Newbery Honor Book Award (runner-up in the Newbery competition) for 1967. Her second book, *From the Mixed-up Files of Mrs. Basil E. Frankweiler*, also published in 1967, won the Newbery Award itself. These are the highest awards earned by U.S. authors of children's books. Given by the "Association for Library Services to Children of the American Library Association," the Newbery Award makes a work an instant classic; the Honor Book Award confers only slightly less prestige.

Since 1968 Konigsburg's books have won more awards than she has kept track of. *Files* also won the 1970 William Allen White Award. Konigsburg herself received the Carnegie-Mellon Merit Award, which goes to authors, not to works, in 1971. The American Library Association Notable Children's Book award went to *A Proud Taste for Scarlet and Miniver* in 1974. *The Second Mrs. Giaconda* and *Father's Arcane Daughter* both received the American Library Association "best book for young adults" award in the years of their publications (1975 and 1976, respectively). And both *Throwing Shadows* and *Up from Jericho Tel* were named American Library Association Notable Children's Books in 1980 and 1987, respectively.

Konigsburg has described her most recent "award" as learning that her work was part of the curriculum of a college course titled "Classical Children's Literature." "I was so pleased to be considered an author of 'classical' children's literature," she says. "I really like the idea that one generation has read my work, and now another generation is reading it. I like the sense of continuity" (Interview, 29 June 1990).

* * *

Elaine Lobl was born in New York City on 10 February 1930 to Beulah and Adolph Lobl. She was the second daughter, Harriett being the elder. The family moved to Phoenixville, Pennsylvania, in 1930, to Youngstown, Ohio, in 1939, and then to Farrell, Pennsylvania, in 1941. (Sherry, the youngest, was born in Farrell.) Konigsburg describes the Pennsylvania towns as "small mill town[s] where there was no one named Jones. . . . Where . . . having a class full of Radasevitches and Gabellas and Zaharious [was] normal" ("NAA," 393). Youngstown, as we will see, was a slightly different matter.

Konigsburg describes her parents as loving and encouraging, but they had no reason to encourage her to be a writer; she showed no interest in writing. "My father encouraged learning, though," Konigsburg reports. "I was an avid reader after first grade" (Interview, 29 June 1990). The Lobls did encourage Elaine as an artist, she adds:

> One day I was supposed to be taking a nap, or something. Instead I went upstairs and drew, copied actually, some comics—I think it was *Li'l Abner* by Al Capp. My mother saw my copies, and she didn't scold me for missing my nap. She praised my drawing. Both my parents praised me for the drawing—and my father ordered a set of oil paints from the Sears catalog, and got me a little wooden easel, and I painted. (Interview, 29 June 1990)

Elaine Lobl attended first through fourth grade and half of fifth grade in Phoenixville, Pennsylvania. When she was nine she and her family moved to Youngstown, Ohio, for a year. There she finished fifth grade at William McKinley Elementary School, which she later enshrined in the title and plot of *Jennifer, Hecate, Macbeth, William McKinley, and Me, Elizabeth.* Times were hard in 1940, and the Lobls needed to find a home with a lower rent. Consequently Elaine and her family had to move to a new home—and a new school district—in Youngstown halfway through her sixth-grade year. Mr. Perkins, the principal of William McKinley, thought it would be better for Elaine if she did not switch schools in mid-year, however. Mr. Perkins asked Beulah Lobl if Elaine could continue to attend William McKinley, coming across town by bus. Mrs. Lobl gave her permission, and Elaine became a bus child—one of two attending William McKinley.

Konigsburg tells a story of her days at William McKinley that will sound familiar to readers of her "Momma at the Pearly Gates" in *Altogether, One at a Time*:

> While I was in sixth grade, I used to go upstairs at lunchtime and draw on the blackboard. Another girl, Roseann Dolores Ansevino, was also being bused to William McKinley—I don't know why. She and I did not get along; in fact, she once called me "a dirty Jew." However, after I drew a giant fly on the blackboard upstairs, she invited everyone to come and admire it. We got to be friendly. (Interview, 29 June 1990)

The anecdote shows Konigsburg's early-appearing talent for drawing. It also parallels closely the later short story, which, says Konigsburg, is the only autobiographical account she has written (Interview, 29 June 1990).

Leaving Youngstown in 1941, the Lobls moved to Farrell, Pennsylvania, another small mill town, like Phoenixville. In Farrell Junior High School Elaine won a War Bond contest with one of her drawings, but art languished in Farrell Senior High, where basketball and marching band were the school's major interests; no art classes were taught. Elaine's art career came to a temporary halt.

Konigsburg's writing career, on the other hand, still had not begun. She did co-edit her senior high newspaper (winning an award for a feature story on the homecoming queen), and she worked on the yearbook, but in Farrell no one thought of her becoming a writer. No one, in fact, thought of anyone's becoming a writer. As Konigsburg later explained it, "In [Farrell], I knew no one who made his living from the arts—I knew no writers, no artists. At that time, a person went away to college to *be* something; you went away to be a teacher, or . . . an engineer, or . . . a chemist. So I went away to be a chemist because I was good at it and that was the sort of thing that you did."[1]

After graduating with top honors from Farrell Senior High School, Elaine Lobl "went away to be a chemist." But first she worked for a year (1947–48) as bookkeeper for the Shenango Valley Provision Company in Sharon, Pennsylvania. The company was co-owned by Leonard Rosenberg, the husband of her older sister, Harriett, and Sidney Konigsburg, who five years later also became her brother-in-law when she married his brother, David. It was during this year's precollege work that Elaine grew to know David Konigsburg. She later said, "For me, it was love at first sight" (Interview, 29 June 1990).

After her year in Sharon, she went to Carnegie Institute of Technology (now Carnegie Mellon University) in Pittsburgh. Her courses were mostly science-oriented, but she says that a nonscience course important to her writing was her freshman English class with Dr. A. Fred Sochatoff: "We were all science students, and in his class we were taught to address complex issues in a straightforward manner . . . and that still stays with me. I still think that's important" (Interview, 29 June 1990).

* * *

Elaine Lobl was reading mostly scientific and textbooks during each school year at Carnegie Mellon; in the summers she read *Scientific American*, to be sure, but also tried to catch up on the classics and read some contemporary works. Her reading in the summer of 1952, following her graduation from Carnegie with a bachelor's degree in chemistry, was the most influential of her reading up to that time:

When I graduated [1952], *The Diary of Ann Frank* had just been published. That book had a major impact on me.

I bought the book on the way to visit my father, who had been hospitalized with an ulcer attack. I gave him the book to read while he was in the hospital. He read it in two days, then gave it to me to read.

That book brought the war closer than anything I had experienced up to that point. It was a simple, basic book, dealing with concrete details and day-to-day living, and it was profound. Apparently, the specific has always been more meaningful to me than the general. For me, reading about the deaths of 6 million people was somehow less heart-breaking than reading about the death of one girl.

I look back now, and I realize that *The Diary of Ann Frank*, and, later, Elie Wiesel's *Night*, impressed me with the way they could touch me deeply by conveying the specifics of action and character. I follow that approach in my writing now. (Interview, 29 June 1990)

A second influence on her writing was, and still is, David Konigsburg. The two dated one another throughout their college years, then married on 6 July 1952. Both worked in research while attending graduate school together at the University of Pittsburgh, Elaine in chemistry and David in psychology. Konigsburg states that David's influence on her writing involves the psychology of her characters: "He read my first books; he checked them for inconsistency of character. He still advises me in that area sometimes; I always accept his advice about psychological matters" (Interview, 29 June 1990).

Konigsburg did not finish her master's degree in chemistry at Pittsburgh. She says of her aborted career as a chemist, "I'm convinced that, had I not been such a disaster in the lab, I could have made a contribution to chemistry, something creative. I had the mind for it, but not the temperament. . . . [T]here was no one to tell me that it is only in the higher reaches that science and art are one" (*CA* interview, 251). Science nonetheless remained a central interest for Konigsburg. After she and David moved to Jacksonville, Florida, in 1954, she taught science in a private girls' school, Bartram School, from 1954 to 1955 (and again after her children were born, from 1960 to 1962). It was at Bartram School that she gained what she describes as an important insight into writing as she prepared for her first class:

It was my first time to teach, and I wanted to give it everything I had. I prepared my first class outline and took it to Miss Olga Pratt, the headmistress. The outline was wonderful—it had philosophy of science, it had history of science, it had everything. Miss Pratt read it through carefully, put it down, paused, looked at me, and said, "Start with water."

She was right, of course. I started with water and the students learned scientific theory and scientific method along the way. The same principle applies to my writing. In all my successful writing, I've been careful to "start with water," with specifics, and in novel writing that means character and plot. The philosophy must percolate through the story, not vice versa.[2]

Chemistry and science, then, influenced Konigsburg's writing from the first.[3]

Teaching chemistry ceased from 1955 to 1959, as another influence on her later writing appeared: the Konigsburgs' three children. Paul was born in 1955, Laurie in 1956, and Ross Adam in 1959. Konigsburg incorporated her children into her works in the illustrations: Laurie, for example, was Claudia's prototype in *From the Mixed-up Files of Mrs. Basil E. Frankweiler* (she later appeared as other characters as well). Perhaps more important were the children's critical roles: Konigsburg read her writing to them after school. "I watched their reactions," she says. "I might change something if their reactions said it wasn't funny, or didn't work" (Interview, 29 June 1990).

Konigsburg's four grandchildren—Samuel Todd, Laurie's child; Amy, Ross's child; Anna, Paul's child; and Sarah, Ross's second child—have also begun to influence her writing. Samuel Todd has become a major part of Konigsburg's two most recent books, as she explains: "Samuel Todd would not say his colors. We thought he might be color blind. So I bought a blank book, and I drew some colored pictures, and I wrote a text, and he liked it—and he liked the colors. And he learned the colors. Laurie showed the book to others, and they liked it, too. That made me brave enough to show it to Jean Karl, my editor. She thought it worked and agreed to publish it" (Interview, 29 June 1990). The book, *Samuel Todd's Book of Great Colors*, features Samuel Todd himself on the cover and among the illustrations. It is a picture book, and of course the illustrations are its heart.

A companion picture book, *Samuel Todd's Book of Great Inventions*, was published in 1991. A new book—*Amy Elizabeth Explores Bloomingdale's*—was in press as this study was published (1992). It is also a picture book but has "considerably more text than the earlier picture books" (Interview, 9 April 1992).

* * *

To be sure, the picture books do not mark a wholly new departure for Konigsburg, as her book illustrations witness. From the first, she has used her illustrations both to expand on the text and "to make *specific* certain parts of the text. For example, I wanted to show the murdered Amy Robsart's bed in *Files*" (Interview, 29 June 1990). Given Konigsburg's emphasis on specifics in her writing, one is not surprised to find her using another of her talents to add to her books' specificity.

Konigsburg's illustrative talent was apparent early in her childhood; she further developed this talent shortly after the birth of her son Ross Adam, when she began to feel she needed to do something not focused on home or children. That feeling led her to take painting lessons in what was then the Adult Education Department of the Jacksonville Art Museum in 1959. Also in 1959 Jacksonville added art to its annual county fair as a competitive division. Konigsburg entered her first painting in that contest in 1959, and it took first place. She entered another painting in the fair's art competition in 1960; it took second place. Then she went back to teaching at Bartram School and had to stop taking painting lessons. Shortly thereafter, when the Konigsburgs decided to move near New York City as the first in a series of career moves for David, Elaine learned from a colleague at Bartram about the Art Students' League in New York City—and she learned that anybody could join. The move completed, she joined.

Their moves took the Konigsburgs first to Saddle Brook, New Jersey, then to Port Chester, New York. These years (1962–67) saw Elaine taking Saturdays off (courtesy of David Konigsburg) to take art lessons in the mornings and to immerse herself in New York City in the afternoons. Also, in 1965, she began to write.

* * *

From 1965 to 1992 Konigsburg has been writing and illustrating predominantly children's literature.[4] Her writing reflects the varied elements of her identity, as revealed in her 1968 description of herself as a "convert from chemistry" ("NAA," 391). In other places she describes herself as a housewife,[5] adding that she has "always loved language" (Jones interview, 181). She is an amalgam of chemist, wife, mother, grandmother, illustrator, and writer.

Elaine and David Konigsburg live alongside a beach near Jacksonville, Florida, where Elaine takes her grandchildren walking on the beach and searching for fossilized sharks' teeth. She has just finished her third picture book, and goes to her office in her home every morning to research, write, and revise—and to review her extensive files. She is also active in her community, serving in 1990–91, for example, on the "Art Venture Fund," which subsidizes rising artists, and as a board member for Jacksonville's Women's Network.

Hers is a busy life that shows no sign of becoming less busy. Her husband, David, retired as of January 1991; when asked about her own retirement, Elaine responds, "I don't want to retire. I'll see what happens. I won't do anything I don't enjoy. Time is finite—I want to spend it doing things I love with people I love" (Interview, 29 June 1990).

2

Moving Inside the Outsiders

Though published in the same year (1967), *Jennifer, Hecate, Macbeth, William McKinley, and Me, Elizabeth* and *From the Mixed-up Files of Mrs. Basil E. Frankweiler* seem at first to have little in common. Like each of Konigsburg's books, plot and characterization are unique. The books do share a setting at least initially in the suburbs, however, and a similar theme. Konigsburg handles the theme differently in both books, but it is the one she has identified as her chief thematic interest: a child's achieving her/his own identity.

Jennifer, Hecate, Macbeth, William McKinley, and Me, Elizabeth

The Plot

The plot for *Jennifer* originated in the Konigsburgs' move to Port Chester, New York, in 1963. Konigsburg's daughter, Laurie, did not at first make friends at her new school. Some weeks after the term started, Laurie asked to go to a friend's house. The friend was black; she became the basis for the Jennifer of Konigsburg's book.

Jennifer's setting is typically suburban, as appears in Elizabeth's description of her home: "Our new town was not full of apartments. . . . There were only three apartment buildings as big as ours. All three sat on the top of the hill from the train station. Hundreds of men rode the train to New York City every morning and rode it home every night. My father did."[1]

Elizabeth leaves her apartment building one morning, walking alone to her new school, the William McKinley Elementary School, in which she is still an outsider. On the way she meets Jennifer, who coolly announces, "I'm a witch" (*J*, 6). Elizabeth, intrigued, follows up on this surprising announcement and becomes convinced of its truth as Jennifer seems to work magic (such as providing a watermelon in January [71–72]). Elizabeth becomes Jennifer's apprentice, then a "journeyman witch" (*J*, 76). The two girls spend a great deal of time together, some of it devoted to magical incantations in their "magic circle" in the park (*J*, 28) but much of it spent in talk about Elizabeth's daily life and Jennifer's reading. Aside from her reading interests, Jennifer does not talk about a normal, little-girl life—only about life as a witch.

Elizabeth does not tell her parents about Jennifer. In fact, she does not tell anyone that Jennifer has become her friend, nor do the two show their friendship to others at William McKinley. They are allied in a secret relationship that Elizabeth cherishes, in part for its very secrecy. That relationship of witch and aspiring witch climaxes and ends when the major spell they are to work together involves dropping a live toad into a boiling cauldron. Neither can stomach this act, but Jennifer manipulates Elizabeth so that it is Elizabeth, rather than Jennifer, who ruins the spell. Elizabeth, at first furious at Jennifer for being willing to boil the toad, becomes more furious as she realizes Jennifer never intended to boil it. She walks away, "dismissed" as a journeyman witch (*J*, 106–7). She does not see Jennifer for two weeks.

Then, left alone one Saturday morning as her mother goes shopping, Elizabeth looks out the window at the neighboring estate (with greenhouse) and realizes the greenhouse is the only place Jennifer could have found their toad at this season (March). Moreover, the only place Jennifer could have found a watermelon in January must have been the greenhouse. Jennifer's magic suddenly becomes a matter of location, not incantation, and Elizabeth realizes Jennifer must live on the estate and that her father must work in the greenhouse. Just as she reasons her way through these facts, someone knocks on the apartment door. It is Jennifer, who makes a joke of her former witchery, then joins Elizabeth in laughing at the joke. It was "the first time we laughed together" (*J*, 116), reports Elizabeth. That first laugh begins a normal friendship between the two girls. The book closes as that friendship develops.

Jennifer's being a "witch" is the hinge on which the plot depends. It is not until the book's close, when Elizabeth reasons her way through two pieces of "magic," that both Elizabeth and the reader realize that Jennifer has been presenting a cleverly crafted illusion. The plot walks a line between fantasy and reality, Elizabeth remaining solidly real and Jennifer seeming to have fantastic powers.

The Characters

Elizabeth embraces Jennifer's witchcraft and the chance to become an apprentice witch. Both children adopt witchcraft as a response to their "outsider" situations: Elizabeth has just come to William McKinley Elementary School and is not yet socially assimilated; Jennifer is black—the only black child in her school.

Elizabeth, the narrator, describes her outsider status early in the story: "I always walked the back road to school, and I always walked alone. We had moved to the apartment house in town in September just before school started, and I walked alone because I didn't have anyone to walk with" (*J*, 3). Moreover, Elizabeth, an only child, lacks siblings as well as friends.

Jennifer is also an outsider, though the skin color that gives rise to her outsider status is, interestingly, not immediately apparent in the book. When Elizabeth first sees Jennifer, she notes that she is wearing a Halloween costume like her own—a Pilgrim dress. She notes further only that Jennifer's foot, hanging from the low branch Jennifer is sitting on, is surprisingly bony. One does not learn of Jennifer's blackness until one sees the illustration on p. 19, and perhaps not then.[2]

Elizabeth establishes Jennifer's outsider status after the two arrive at school together on the first day of their association.

Elizabeth reports that two other girls "were both whispering and giggling. Probably about Jennifer" (*J,* 14). At that point, the reader does not know *why* the two might be doing this, but that it is happening is the first suggestion of Jennifer's loner status in the school.

Jennifer's response to her situation as a black appears in her first words to Elizabeth, who has just said, "You're going to lose that shoe" (*J,* 6). Jennifer replies, "Witches never lose anything" (*J,* 6). Elizabeth's surprised and challenging "But you're not a witch" prompts Jennifer's "I won't argue with you. . . . But I'll tell you this much. . . . Just because I don't have on a silly black costume and carry a silly broom and wear a silly black hat, doesn't mean that I'm not a witch. I'm a witch all the time and not just on Halloween" (*J,* 6). Jennifer has become an outsider by choice; instead of allowing others to reject her because she is black, she has chosen to become a witch.

Both to Elizabeth and to the reader Jennifer's witchhood soon becomes credible. During the girls' first meeting Jennifer identifies the cookies in Elizabeth's bag as chocolate chip, leaving Elizabeth wondering how Jennifer could tell. Elizabeth also notes that Jennifer's Pilgrim costume appears authentic, even "ancient" (*J,* 7). Later, at school, Elizabeth receives from Jennifer a note written in an antique script; then, on the Saturday following their first meeting, Jennifer chants a "spell" most impressively and leads Elizabeth through a ritual in a "magic circle" (*J,* 28–29). Elizabeth accepts, at least tentatively, Jennifer's claim to be a witch.

As the preceding has begun to suggest, Konigsburg characterizes these two primarily through their interaction. Jennifer, for example, tells only Elizabeth that she is a witch. Elizabeth, moreover, mentions Jennifer's status, and her own "apprentice" status, to no one. The two do their witchcraft only in one another's company. As time goes by, however, their relationship shows promise of growing beyond the narrow, even restrictive, bounds of witchcraft.

For example, after one of their regular visits to the library the two go to the park, march three times around their "magic circle," then talk: "We talked about witches in colonial days and the man who liked to hang witches in colonial days: Cotton

Mather. We talked about plants that eat insects: insectivo-
rous. . . . We talked about the guillotine in France, . . . about lice
and the bubonic plague, and other interesting things" (*J*, 36).
Konigsburg, in short, establishes the two girls as "witches" together, but she also takes some pains to show the beginnings of
a fruitful relationship outside the fantastic. That growing
relationship, and the increasing tension of the contrasting relationship of "witch" and "apprentice witch," quickly establishes
one of the major themes of the book.

Themes

Konigsburg has said that her chief theme in all her writings is
that of a "middle-aged child" finding his or her identity. *Jennifer*
establishes a false identity early in the book, and Elizabeth accepts it—even joins in it. The two reach an impasse, as one
might expect: their relationship cannot grow past a certain point
if they persist in the false "witch" identities.[3] Konigsburg shows
this as the two girls reach the climax of their witchery: they are
to make a "flying ointment," rub it on, and fly.

The ointment would not allow them to fly, of course, any
more than their false witchery will allow their relationship to
grow. So Jennifer manipulates Elizabeth into spoiling the magic
ointment, which could easily mark the end of their relationship.
Instead, it signals the beginning of a relationship no longer
based on a lie. After Elizabeth reasons out where Jennifer and
her family must live, Jennifer (almost magically) appears at
Elizabeth's door. The two reconcile in laughter—the first time
Jennifer has laughed throughout the book. The book closes:

> For the first time we laughed together. . . . Now we laugh together
> a lot. We walk to school together, too. Sometimes I play at her
> house. . . .
>   Neither of us pretends to be a witch any more. Now we mostly
> enjoy being what we really are . . . just Jennifer and just
> me . . . just good friends. (*J*, 116–17)

Having arrived at "just Jennifer and just me," Elizabeth has
moved beyond her outsider status, and beyond her "apprentice
witch" status; she is now "me" and Jennifer is "Jennifer." The

two have established both their own identities and a relationship that can grow as they enjoy "being what we really are."

Secrecy is another theme. As will become more fully apparent in *Files*, Konigsburg feels that secrets are important. Thus
Elizabeth notes about the witchcraft she shares with Jennifer,
"No one knew that we were witch and apprentice or that we
even knew each other. Witchcraft is a private affair. Very private. It's secret" (*J*, 44–45). Later Elizabeth adds, "It feels
wonderful to have a secret. Sometimes I thought I wanted our
secret to be discovered accidentally, but I didn't want to share
Jennifer with the entire fifth grade" (*J*, 53).

The third theme in *Jennifer*, the most subtly stated of the
three, concerns black-white relations. Konigsburg does not
comment on this theme in the book; in fact, as I've noted, one
does not realize Jennifer is black until late in the book. Thus at
first we believe we are reading a story about two white girls,
loners, getting to know one another and thus shedding their
aloneness. That belief persists until we have become involved
with both girls; then we realize Jennifer is black.

The effect? Very subtly, Konigsburg leads us to ignore the
issue of skin color. Or, perhaps better, Konigsburg leads us to
realize color ought not be an issue. Presumably Jennifer would
not be a loner if she were not black, but this is not apparent at
first. Readers know only that other children giggle at and about
her and that she maintains an air of proud self-sufficiency.
Readers probably take her "witch" status as sufficient explanation for her loner status. Instead, one finally concludes that
Jennifer has adopted the witch status as a defense against being
rejected because of her color. When Elizabeth rejects her, it is
not because she is black. At that point Jennifer sees that she
need not be an outsider to Elizabeth because of being black. She
can then drop her witchery and be "just Jennifer."[4]

An interesting contrast appears in another children's book
with interracial characters published in the same year as *Jennifer*: Zilpha Keatley Snyder's *The Egypt Game*. Here the
"outsider," April, is white; her accepting friend, Melanie, is
black. Unlike the case in *Jennifer*, however, black and white
have little to do with characterization or theme. The book has
simply been integrated.

Style

The preceding discussion of plot, characterization, and themes may suggest why *Jennifer* has been popular. The story is interesting and fast-paced, the characters at the same time credible and (until the close) fantastic, and the themes profound. The style with which Konigsburg presents these elements of her book makes them effective. That style is light, witty, and respectful of the reader, setting a standard Konigsburg follows in all her works.

Part of the strength of Konigsburg's style appears in her use of descriptive detail. Consider, for example, the passage in which Elizabeth describes the woods she walks through on her way to school: "The footsteps of [other children] for ten years had worn away the soil so that the roots of the trees were bare and made steps for walking up and down the steep slope" (*J,* 4). Every reader who has taken a path through woods will recognize these root steps.

Humor is another major element of Konigsburg's style. One of its chief manifestations is the witty use of words, as when Elizabeth characterizes herself as a "fussy eater" (*J,* 33), saying about her not eating eggs, "Even when I was a little baby before I knew better, I knew better" (*J,* 34). Some of the most humorous parts of the book involve Elizabeth's great-uncle and great-aunt, whom she styles collectively "the Greats." Her descriptions of their speaking habits (they converse only in questions) and of their exotic health-food diet are very funny. An example of her recounting of "the Greats" and their habits comes from the night the Greats agree to be her baby-sitters:

> I have never been so well baby-sat. The Greats laid out my pajamas and folded down the covers of my cot. They filled the bathtub for me and checked the temperature of the water. . . . After I got to bed, both of them came into the bedroom every half hour to check me. It was almost impossible to go to sleep. They kept covering me. Every part of me was covered except those parts I needed for breathing. (*J,* 70–71)

Konigsburg's respect for her readers—which I consider an element of her style—appears in her inclusion of a Shakespearean element in her novel. It appears when Jennifer not only produces a toad in March, to Elizabeth's amazement, but also announces that "Witches always have toads" and then recites the "Round about the cauldron go" speech of the three witches in *Macbeth* (*J*, 95). Jennifer is not only interested in the witches as witches, but she understands that what they presented to Macbeth was trouble—a warning. Jennifer elaborates, "They told him the truth in such a way that he got to feeling too sure of himself" (*J*, 96). Jennifer then advises Elizabeth to read *Macbeth*. Such a passage shows Konigsburg's considerable respect for the abilities of her 8- to 14-year-old readers.

Comparable Fiction

Witch stories of the Halloween variety are common in children's literature. Less common are stories that separate witchery from Halloween and deal more or less seriously with the topic. One of the serious witch stories is Margaret Mahy's *The Haunting* (1982), in which Barney Scholar—still in "primary school" and apparently aged about 10—seems to be becoming a male witch, or magician. His mysterious Uncle Cole already is a magician, and so is his sister Tory. A reader does not doubt that this book is fantastic; there is never the "perhaps, perhaps not" question we meet in *Jennifer*.

Konigsburg seems at first to be writing a tale like *The Haunting* in *Jennifer*. She never quite crosses the line into fantasy, though, thanks to Elizabeth's authenticity. Part of the appeal of *Jennifer* is not being sure whether or not one is reading fantasy—just as Elizabeth is not quite sure Jennifer is a witch.

Not actually a witch story, *Jennifer* compares more closely with children's books that address black-white relations. Books with this theme are still rare, though some began to see print following the appearance in 1965 of Nancy Larrick's "The All-White World of Children's Books."[5] One such book is, as I've noted, Snyder's *The Egypt Game*, although Snyder does not address the relationship between black girl and white girl as a racial issue.

A book in which the black-white relationship *is* central is

Bruce Brooks's *The Moves Make the Man* (1984), which at first seems to focus on playing basketball. The book is actually about caring, both within a black family and between a remarkably good (black) basketball player and the white youth he teaches to play basketball. Here, black and white are explicitly central to the plot and characterization as well as to the theme—Brooks does not seek the understated, even unstated, delicacy of *Jennifer*.

From the Mixed-up Files of Mrs. Basil E. Frankweiler

The Plot

Like *Jennifer*, *Files* involves the suburban child's search for identity; the approach, however, is quite different. *Files* begins in a New York suburb (Greenwich) and returns to that setting at the close. The intervening setting, however, is the Metropolitan Museum of Art in New York City. The search for identity, moreover, involves not "outsider" children but children thoroughly adjusted to their surroundings.

The plot of *Files* grew from an actual incident—the purchase of a statue for $225 by the Metropolitan Museum of Art, as reported in the 26 October 1965 *New York Times*. The statue was thought "possibly the work of Leonardo da Vinci or of his teacher."[6] Konigsburg took the story as a plot element but changed da Vinci to Michelangelo, both because she admired Michelangelo and because at that time she had a grudge against da Vinci.[7] She also changes the statue: in *Files* it is an angel; in reality it is *The Lady with the Primroses* (Townsend, 123).

Two of Konigsburg's personal experiences also went into *Files*: one was reading a book telling of children captured by pirates, in which the children dropped their "thin veneer of civilization" and became pirates themselves; the other was a family picnic at Yellowstone National Park. Lacking picnic table or benches, she and her family crouched on the ground.

> Then the complaints began: the chocolate milk was getting warm, and there were ants over everything, and the sun was melting the

icing on the cupcakes. This was hardly having to rough it, and yet
my small group could think of nothing but the discomfort. . . .
    Where, I wondered, would they ever consider running to if they
ever left home? They certainly would never consider any place
less elegant than the Metropolitan Museum of Art.[8]

Thus, combining the newspaper account of the statue, the pirate
story, and her children's response to al fresco dining, Konigsburg wrote of Claudia and Jamie and their running away to the
Metropolitan Museum of Art.

Files opens in a rush. Feeling ill used, Claudia decides to
run away, but not alone. In need of both company and money for
this endeavor, she recruits her younger brother Jamie to run
away with her. Jamie is "rich"; he saves every penny he gets.
Pursuing Claudia's plan, and in keeping with Konigsburg's interest in recounting the ways of suburban life, Claudia and
Jamie catch the Greenwich 10:42 local to New York City. Once
they arrive in New York, the two walk to the Metropolitan
Museum of Art and calmly take up residence, visiting various
galleries by day and sleeping in a sixteenth-century bed—"scene
of the alleged murder of Amy Robsart"[9]—by night.

Just as this idyllic existence might have started to pall, the
children learn that for $225 the Metropolitan Museum of Art
has acquired a statue, *Angel,* whose sculptor is unknown but
thought possibly to have been Michelangelo. The statue could
thus be worth millions; it has become a nine-days'-wonder.
Claudia decides that she and Jamie ought to try to solve the
mystery of its sculptor. Claudia is not sure why she wants to
solve the mystery, but feels that the statue "would do something
important to her" (*F,* 65).

Since the two children cannot investigate *Angel* during the
day, they concentrate on her during their nights in the museum.
They discover a stone mason's mark characteristic of Michelangelo and think they have solved the mystery. To their disap-
pointment, the museum officials had also discovered the mark
but ruled it inconclusive, as other non-Michelangelo statues also
bear this mark.

Jamie, philosophical about their failure to solve the mystery,
is ready to return home to Greenwich. Claudia, however, cannot

Claudia shows Jamie their bed—the bed in which Amy Robsart, first wife of Lord Robert Dudley, was allegedly murdered. *From the Mixed-up Files of Mrs. Basil E. Frankweiler* (New York: Atheneum, 1967), 37.

bear the idea. "We've accomplished nothing," she sobs (*F*, 117), and tells Jamie, "We need to make more of a discovery . . . [about *Angel* because] I want to go back to Greenwich different" (*F*, 118–19). She cannot articulate her feelings any more clearly, but they are very strong—so strong that she insists Jamie and she travel to the home of Mrs. Basil E. Frankweiler, donor of the statue to the Metropolitan Museum of Art, to see if she can solve the mystery.

Mrs. Frankweiler could solve the mystery, but she does not. Instead, she allows the children one hour to seek the answer to the mystery in her "mixed-up files." In their last six minutes, they find it, and Claudia now has what she sought. Mrs. Frankweiler explains why this answer is so important to Claudia: "It will enable her to return to Greenwich *different*" (*F*, 149). Moreover, she will be different "on the inside where it counts" (*F*, 150). Though Claudia did not know it, it is this inside difference, this secret, that she has been seeking. Having found it, she happily returns with Jamie to her suburban home.

Even so bare an outline may serve to point out the interest of the book's plot. Several particularly appealing plot devices deserve special mention:

1. Running away, not "from" home but "to" the Metropolitan Museum of Art.

2. Hiding from the museum guards in the men's and women's rooms by standing on the toilets. As Claudia describes it while telling Jamie how to do it, "Feet up. Head down. Door open. . . . Because I'm certain that when they check the ladies' room and the men's room, they peek under the door and check only to see if there are feet" (*F*, 36).[10]

3. The children's supporting themselves financially while staying in the museum: they not only depend on Jamie's hoarded wealth, but they take money by night from the museum restaurant's fountain pool. Because every child dreams of taking the temptingly visible money from such pools, this device is particularly appealing to Konigsburg's readers.

The Characters

Characterization is as major an element in *Files* as it is in *Jennifer*. Both Claudia and Jamie are strong characters; they are also very different characters.

As appears in the book's first paragraph, Claudia "didn't like discomfort; even picnics were untidy and inconvenient. . . . Therefore, she decided that her leaving home would not be just running from somewhere but would be running to somewhere" (*F*, 5). She wants to run away because she feels she is "subject to a lot of injustice" in her suburban home; she is the oldest and the only female child, and thus gets stuck with household chores "while her brothers got out of everything" (*F*, 7). The book's narrator, the Mrs. Basil E. Frankweiler of the title, adds that Claudia is bored at "the monotony of everything" (*F*, 7).

Though Konigsburg could thus far be characterizing Everygirl, Claudia soon takes on the dimensions of a character all her own. For example, she enjoys planning her running away; she researches it carefully, using maps of New York City, "some pamphlets about the museum" (*F*, 8–9), and even an American Automobile Association Tourguide. Moreover, she has human weaknesses: faced with a special on hot fudge sundaes, she buys one even though it will delay her running away.

Part of Claudia's characterization is her choice of Jamie to run away with her. She feels she can count on Jamie to keep their secret; he is "good for a laugh" every so often and—on a practical note—is "rich." We also note that Jamie is Claudia's "second youngest" brother and therefore presumably more manipulable than the older one. Claudia is a planner.

She is also something of a worrier, as we learn early in the book when she is crouching down in the back of her school bus: "She didn't like keeping her head down so long. Perspiration was causing her cheek to stick to the plastic seat; she was convinced that she would develop a medium-serious skin disease within five minutes after she got off the bus" (*F*, 21). She sounds equally the hypochondriac as she approaches her first bedtime in the Metropolitan Museum of Art: "It was much earlier than her bedtime at home, but still Claudia felt tired. She thought she might have an iron deficiency anemia: tired blood" (*F*, 41).

This concern for her health likewise appears in her refusal to consider hitchhiking to New York: "Hitchhike? and take a chance of getting kidnapped or robbed? Or we could even get mugged" (*F*, 24), she replies to Jamie's suggestion.

She has considerably more than fussbudget stature, though, as becomes evident when Jamie challenges her authority and her planning, saying he does not want to "hide out in" the Metropolitan Museum of Art. Instead of confronting Jamie's opposition head-on, she buys him off: "Claudia appointed him treasurer; he would not only hold all the money, he would also keep track of it and pass judgment on all expenditures. Then Jamie began to feel that the Metropolitan offered several advantages and would provide adventure enough" (*F*, 27). Much of Claudia's characterization, in fact, appears in her relationship with Jamie.

A major element of their relationship is Claudia's constantly correcting Jamie's grammar and wording. Thus when she first starts to tell him of her plan (and breaks up his ongoing card game to do so), Jamie complains, "'What's the matter with you, Claude? First you bust up my card game, then you don't tell me [what you want]. It's undecent.' 'Break up, not bust up. Indecent, not undecent,' Claudia corrected" (*F*, 13). Claudia continues such corrections throughout the book, even though Jamie suggests late in the book that she quit "ending every single discussion with an argument about grammar," to which she responds with surprising humility, "I'll try" (*F*, 119). Humility is not a constant for Claudia, however. For example, she decides that she and Jamie should learn everything about the Metropolitan Museum of Art and outlines daily lessons for them. Even if a fussbudget, Claudia earns a reader's respect for her grand plans.

As the book proceeds, we see that the chief element of Claudia's character is her desire to go home a different person from the one who ran away from home. Konigsburg presents this desire as actually changing Claudia's character. This appears most clearly when Claudia insists that she and Jamie go to Connecticut to visit the former owner of *Angel*, Mrs. Basil E. Frankweiler. "I just have a hunch she'll see us and that she knows [the answer to the mystery of *Angel*]," Claudia explains. Jamie responds, "I've never known you to have a hunch before,

Claudia. You usually plan everything" (*F,* 122). Claudia has changed. The careful planner of the opening pages has become a girl who insists upon following a hunch.

Her hunch is correct, too, as Mrs. Frankweiler points out. Mrs. Frankweiler first explains what is troubling Claudia—"that running away from home didn't make a real difference" (*F,* 138). She then provides Claudia the chance to solve the mystery of *Angel.* Claudia (and Jamie) do solve the mystery, establishing to their own satisfaction who sculpted the statue. Mrs. Frankweiler binds both Jamie and Claudia to keeping their new knowledge secret—and Claudia finds having a secret is what she needed. She was seeking a separate identity of her own, and the statue has made it possible for her to have that identity. She has found the kind of difference she needs: "Secrets are safe, and they do much to make you different. On the inside where it counts" (*F,* 150). Her identity established, Claudia can now go home. The book ends as she and Jamie return to their parents.

Though Claudia is pre-eminent, Jamie's characterization is important in *Files.* Jamie is Konigsburg's first male character. (Males barely figure in *Jennifer.*) From his first appearance, Konigsburg makes him distinct from Claudia. Where Claudia is penniless as the book opens and must save her allowance and scrounge a train ticket in order to support her part in the running away, Jamie has saved "almost every penny" (*F,* 5–6) he ever received. It later appears that Jamie has saved the sum of $24.43, largely from his winnings at the ongoing card game of "War," which he plays on the school bus with his friend Bruce. Jamie usually wins at this game, but then Jamie cheats. He has, in fact, "cheated Bruce through all second grade and through all third grade so far" (*F,* 34), as he blurts out to Claudia when she slights his card-playing ability.

Jamie has a sense of humor as well as acquisitive instincts. Responding to Claudia's direction to leave his trumpet out of the case Wednesday and instead pack the case with "as much clean underwear as possible and socks and at least one other shirt" (*F,* 14–15), Jamie says, "All in a trumpet case? I should have taken up the bass fiddle" (*F,* 15).

Jamie is in many ways the ideal co-conspirator; as he announces, he likes "complications" (*F,* 17), and Claudia's plan to run away is highly complicated. He also possesses typical little-boy characteristics, as appears when he enters the Metropolitan Museum of Art and has to wear his ski jacket so the bagged-down condition of his trousers will not be apparent (his $24.43 is all in change, and it pulls his trousers down below his waist). Wearing the ski jacket indoors, he gets hot: "Claudia would never have permitted herself to become so overheated, but Jamie liked perspiration, a little bit of dirt, and complications" (*F,* 33).

Jamie's monied condition also makes him the treasurer for the expedition. His veto power is extensive, and a constant irritation to Claudia. Thus, upon their arrival in New York City, Jamie refuses to authorize their spending money for a cab to the Metropolitan Museum of Art, or even for a bus: "No bus. We'll walk" (*F,* 28–29). Claudia decides Jamie is not only a gambler but "a cheapskate" (*F,* 29).

Like Claudia, Jamie changes as a result of the experiences he and his sibling share. Just after he tells Claudia he has never before known her to have a hunch—she usually plans everything in detail—he simply, and swiftly, agrees with her request that they spend the bulk of their remaining money to go visit Mrs. Frankweiler. Claudia is amazed: "That's a first for you, too," she observes. Jamie asks what she means, and she explains the "first" is "buying something without asking the price first" (*F,* 122–23). In short, and as this incident shows, much of the characterization of the two children appears in their interaction.

The two define each other also in their constant arguments about "grammar," as Jamie calls it. The funniest such passage appears early in the story. Jamie tells Claudia he needs the compass he brought to find their way "out of the woods" (*F,* 23).

"What woods?" Claudia asked.

"The woods we'll be hiding out in," Jamie answered.

"Hiding *out in*? What kind of language is that?"

"English language. That's what kind."

"Who ever told you that we were going to hide out in the woods?" Claudia demanded.

"There! You said it. You said it!" Jamie shrieked.

"Said what? I never said we're going to hide out in the woods."

Now Claudia was yelling, too.
    "No! you said *'hide out in.'*"
    "I did not!"
    Jamie exploded. "You did, too. You said, 'Who ever told you that we're going to *hide out in* the woods?' You said that."
    "O.K. O.K." Claudia replied. . . . "O.K.," she repeated. "I *may* have said *hide out in*, but I didn't say *the woods*."
    "Yes sir. You said, 'Who ever told you that . . .'"
    Claudia didn't give him a chance to finish. "I know. I know. Now let's begin by my saying that we are going to hide out in the Metropolitan Museum of Art in New York City."
    Jamie said, "See! See! you said it again."
    "I did not! I said, 'The Metropolitan Museum of Art.'"
    "You said *hide out in* again."
    "All right. Let's forget the English language lessons. We are going to the Metropolitan Museum of Art in Manhattan." (*F*, 23–24)

The passage illustrates perfectly the interaction of two siblings, each clever, each argumentative, each determined to get his/her way.

Less fully characterized than Claudia and Jamie, but a constant presence, is the narrator, Mrs. Basil E. Frankweiler. She opens the book: Konigsburg's drawing of her sitting at a desk in front of her files, writing a letter, follows the title page. The first page of text is that letter, addressed "To my lawyer, Saxonberg" (*F*, 3). The entire book, in fact, is an account Mrs. Frankweiler writes to Saxonberg to explain "certain changes I want made in my last will and testament" (*F*, 3). The account rehearses Claudia and Jamie's adventures, which Mrs. Frankweiler learns from them while they visit her to learn the secret of *Angel.*

Mrs. Frankweiler is a parenthetical presence throughout the book—that is, she injects her own comments parenthetically, in a distinctly different voice from those of Jamie and Claudia, as she recounts their adventure in the third person. Such an example is her comment on Jamie's feeling flattered by Claudia's "choosing" him to run away with her: "(Flattery is as important a machine as the lever, isn't it, Saxonberg? Give it a proper place to rest, and it can move the world)" (*F*, 14).

We learn details about Mrs. Frankweiler as Claudia reads a newspaper account of *Angel:* "The statue was acquired by the

Parke-Bernet Galleries from the collection of Mrs. Basil E. Frankweiler. . . . Mr. Frankweiler . . . died in 1947. Mrs. Frankweiler now lives on her country estate in Farmington, Connecticut. . . . The Frankweilers had no children" (*F*, 59–60). Her having "had no children" appears as a motivation for Mrs. Frankweiler's acerbic kindness to the two children when they visit her at her Connecticut mansion. She tells them that she would like to experience "one new thing. And that one thing is impossible." After thinking this over, they realize that the 82-year-old woman is saying that she would like to experience motherhood, but it is too late. That means little to them—perhaps little to most child readers—but to an adult reader it is a major characterizing touch.

Aside from the beginning and end of the book, Mrs. Frankweiler does not appear in the action. Her regular parenthetical additions, however, make her a constant presence.

Themes

Mrs. Frankweiler, in fact, states one of the book's major themes: the need for secrets, or at least the need for being "different on the inside." As she narrates Claudia and Jamie's actions, she says concerning Claudia's desire to solve the statue's mystery: "it . . . would do something important to her, though what this was, she didn't quite know" (*F*, 65). Claudia tries to state the importance of the statue's secret when she tells Jamie, "I want to go back [home] different" (*F*, 119). Mrs. Frankweiler later observes that the secret of who sculpted the statue is exactly what Claudia needs: "It will enable her to return to Greenwich *different*" (*F*, 149). She adds, "Claudia doesn't want adventure. . . . Secrets are the kind of adventure she needs. Secrets are safe, and they do much to make you different. On the inside where it counts" (*F*, 150). *Angel* has been important to Claudia, as Claudia thought she could be; the statue's secret becomes a permanent difference Claudia can cherish within herself.

Like Claudia, Jamie comes to see the importance of secrets. As the two children drive back to their suburban home, he tells Claudia, "Let's visit her every time we save enough money. We won't tell anyone. . . . We'll just tell Mom and Dad that we're going bowling" (*F*, 159). Claudia says that Mrs. Frankweiler will "become our grandmother" (*F,* 160), and Jamie adds, "And that will be our secret that we won't even share with her" (*F,* 160). Jamie, too, has grown in the course of the book's adventures.

The theme of difference "on the inside where it counts" is important to this book, and important to Konigsburg. It is not her only theme in *Files,* however. Sibling relationships—even "love," as the Frankweiler narrator observes early on—constitute another major theme. Claudia has just shown Jamie the bed they'll sleep in, the scene of a murder:

> Jamie couldn't control his smile. He said, "You know, Claude, for a sister and fussbudget, you're not too bad."
>
> Claudia replied, "You know, Jamie, for a brother and a cheapskate, you're not too bad."
>
> Something happened at precisely that moment. . . .
>
> What happened was: they became a team, a family of two. There had been times before they ran away when they had acted like a team, but those were very different from *feeling* like a team. . . . [F]eeling like part of a team is something that happens invisibly. You might call it *caring*. You could even call it *love*. (*F,* 38–39)

This theme of sibling love is important to *Files,* but Konigsburg does not belabor it. Having stated it here through her narrator, she does not explicitly return to it.

The reader is now sensitized to the idea of sibling love, though, and sees it throughout the rest of the book—for example, in the debate over whether or not to go to Mrs. Frankweiler's home in Connecticut. Claudia has her hunch that they should go there to find the secret she craves. Jamie, showing by his comment on "hunches" that he sees the importance of the matter to Claudia, agrees immediately, "without asking the price first" (*F,* 123). Because Jamie has exercised his treasurer's veto on most of Claudia's suggestions, his immediate "yes" stands out here—and it underlines his caring, his love, for his sister.

Style

Style is a more complex issue in *Files* than it was in *Jennifer.* The use of a third-person narrator instead of the first-person narrator is perhaps the first element of style the reader notices; Konigsburg's wit and outright poetic use of words also deserve note.

The third-person narrator is Mrs. Frankweiler, who presents the story as a letter she sends to her lawyer, Saxonberg. She begins her letter as the story opens, and the last three pages conclude it. John Rowe Townsend has questioned the use of the Frankweiler narrator, suggesting she comes between action and reader (Townsend, 116).[11] Granted, Mrs. Frankweiler is omnipresent; readers are aware of her at particular moments (though they often forget her). But the question is whether the narrative device works.

To answer that question, we can begin by noting that the Frankweiler narrator actually produces three levels of narration: 1) the actions of Claudia and Jamie, where we forget Frankweiler; 2) the straightforward descriptive comments by an omniscient narrator; and 3) the often-acerbic comments by Mrs. Frankweiler speaking in her own person. For an example:

1. The level of the children

Claudia needed an argument. . . . "Don't you realize that we must try to be inconspicuous?" she demanded of her brother.

"What's inconspicuous?"

"Un-noticeable."

Jamie looked all around. "I think you're brilliant, Claude. New York is a great place to hide out. No one notices no one."

"Anyone," Claudia corrected. She looked at Jamie and found him smiling. She softened. . . . [B]eing called brilliant had cooled her down. (*F*, 30–31)

2. The level of narrative exposition and

3. The (parenthetical) Frankweiler interjection

By the time Claudia and Jamie reached their destination, it was one o'clock, and the museum was busy. On any ordinary Wednesday over 26,000 people come. . . . Tourists visit the museum on Wednesdays. You can tell them because the men carry cameras, and the women look as if their feet hurt; they wear high heeled shoes. (I always say that those who wear 'em deserve 'em.) (*F*, 31–32)

In my judgment, the Frankweiler narrator works. Mrs.

Frankweiler generally functions as an omniscient narrator whose presence one simply forgets: one focuses on the children. That is the case for both levels 1 and 2 above. As for her comments in her own person (usually parenthetical), they not only add dry humor to the narration but also prepare us for the meeting of Mrs. Frankweiler and the children at the book's close. The difference between her voice and the voices of the children also reinforces the difference between young and old, inexperienced and experienced, which becomes evident as the book ends. The difference is a valuable element of the book, and it depends wholly on the narrative stance Konigsburg has chosen to use in *Files*.

A second element of Konigsburg's style in *Files* appears in all her books: her wit. Wit is still more constant in *Files* than in *Jennifer*, and wit may well be why this book instead of the other won the Newbery Award. One cannot recount all such instances in *Files*, but a representative sample would have to include the previously quoted "hide out in" passage, plus the following:

> [Jamie is hiding in the Metropolitan Museum of Art men's room, waiting for the museum to close. One night the guard is late, and tension builds.] What was happening? The hardest part was that every corpuscle of Jamie's nine-year-old self was throbbing with readiness to run, and he had to bind up all that energy into a quiet lump. It was like trying to wrap a loose peck of potatoes into a neat four-cornered package. (*F,* 78)

> [When Mrs. Frankweiler first meets the two children, who think themselves anonymous to her, she asks,] "Are you the children who have been missing from Greenwich for a week?" ... They both looked as if their hearts had been pushed through funnels. (*F,* 127)

Metaphors like these powerfully arrest a reader's attention.

We also note the first appearance in *Files* of an element of ribaldry that will reappear in Konigsburg's later works. Jamie and Claudia are discussing the mystery of the *Angel:*

> "What's the difference between an angel and a cupid?" Jamie inquired.
> "Why?" Claudia asked.

"Because there's a lost cupid for sure."
"Angels wear clothes and wings and are Christian. Cupids wear bows and arrows; they are naked and pagan."
"What's pagan?" Jamie asked. "Boy or girl?"
"How would I know?" Claudia answered.
"You said they are naked." (*F*, 73)

The ribaldry is mild, of course.

The third element of Konigsburg's style is her occasionally poetic use of language—as in the passage where Claudia and Jamie are settling into sleep on their first night in the museum: "She lay there in the great quiet of the museum next to the warm quiet of her brother and allowed the soft stillness to settle around them: a comforter of quiet. The silence seeped from their heads to their soles and into their souls. They stretched out and relaxed. . . . Claudia thought now of hushed and quiet words: glide, fur, banana, peace. Even the footsteps of the night watchman added only an accented quarter-note to the silence that had become a hum, a lullaby" (*F*, 41). The movement here from "great quiet" to "warm quiet" to "comforter of quiet" is both inevitable and surprising. The whispering alliteration of the *s* sounds of "soft stillness . . . settle . . . silence seeped . . . soles . . . souls" adds another dimension of sound to the peaceful sense of the passage while Konigsburg puns on "soles" and "souls." The "hushed and quiet words" move cleverly from "glide" to "peace" in a passage whose focus is peace, and the lively rhythm of "ác-cént-ed quárt-er-nóte" moves to the quietly assonant climax of "a hum, a lullaby." One seldom meets in prose a passage in which sound and sense unite so closely.

Comparable Fiction

Since running away is the central plot element in *Files*, other runaway books are logical comparisons. The logic is a bit misleading, to be sure; Konigsburg alone sends her runaways to an art museum. Most children's-book runaways have more utilitarian goals. In Ouida Sebestyen's *Words by Heart* (1979), for example, Lena Sills runs away to seek her father, days overdue to return home. Dicey Tillerman and her three siblings run away from a well-meaning but insensitive kinswoman in order to *find* a home in Cynthia Voigt's *Homecoming* (1981). Claudia, of course, seeks neither father nor home, but self.

In leaving home to find her self Claudia parallels Sam in Jean George's *My Side of the Mountain* (1959).[12] Once Sam proves he can take care of himself in the wilderness—no, once he proves that the capable self he thinks he is is indeed his true self—he can rejoin his parents in New York City, from which he ran away. This book almost directly opposes *Files*; Sam runs from New York City to a considerably less sophisticated setting (a mountain in the wilderness), he takes no sibling with him, and a major theme is that one child by himself can prevail.

Again, Cynthia Voigt's *Homecoming*—and, indeed, her entire series about the Tillerman siblings and their grandmother—deals even more deeply with the theme of sibling bonding, devoting more attention to brother-sister bonding than to the identity theme that also appears in both Voigt and Konigsburg.

Conclusion

Whether her characters are suburban loners or simply suburban—female or male—Konigsburg portrays their successful search for their own identities in *Jennifer* and in *Files*. The theme is profound; Konigsburg's style, characterization, and plot cannot be separated from the theme of identity, but each interacts with it (and with the other themes) to produce delightful fiction. Konigsburg perhaps expressed this blending of elements best as she described her writing goals in her Newbery Award acceptance speech in 1968: "Tell how it is normal to be very comfortable on the outside but very uncomfortable on the inside. Tell how funny it all is. But tell a little something else, too . . . about how you can be a nonconformist and about how you can be an outsider. And tell how you are entitled to a little privacy" ("NAA," 395).

3

Moving Inward

The books following *Jennifer* and *Files* retain a more or less suburban setting. *About the B'nai Bagels* (1969), in fact, is almost aggressively suburban: its plot centers on the formation and training of a Little League baseball team, whose college-age coach commutes from his "Point Baldwin" home to New York University. *(George)* (1970), however, is set in "Lawton Beach" on the southeastern coast of Florida, a town whose resemblance to Fort Lauderdale—it attracts college students on spring break—is important to the story's plot.

About the B'nai Bagels

The Plot

Bagels begins with the protagonist and narrator, 12-year-old Mark Setzer, telling how his mother, Bessie, came to be the manager of the B'nai B'rith neighborhood Little League team, known to its players as the "B'nai Bagels." Mark then tells of his older brother, Spencer, being dragooned into coaching the team. Mark feels he will probably become a favored member of the team because his mother and brother are running it. To his dismay, he comes to feel that his brother and mother lean over backward *not* to favor him.

In the course of the book one also reads of Mark's preparation for his upcoming bar mitzvah, of his growing skill as a baseball player, of his growing interest in females, of his problems with anti-Semitism, and of his troubled relationship with his former best friend, Herschel Miller. The book closes with the deciding game of the season, which the B'nai Bagels must win to become champions in their league. They win the game, but Mark discovers that the win took place through cheating. He mopes for two days, then discloses the cheat. The Bagels forfeit their championship. Soon thereafter, Mark celebrates his bar mitzvah.

The plotting in *Bagels* is both simple and complex. The simplicity is chronological: Konigsburg locates her story between late March and late August, the Little League baseball season. Two months of preparation and training (late March to early May) precede the season (mid-May to mid-July); Mark delivers a coda in late August. More than ball games, though, takes place inside that chronological envelope.

Perhaps the major nonbaseball event is Mark's bar mitzvah. On the level of both plotting and theme, Konigsburg makes the preparations for and achievement of Mark's bar mitzvah parallel his preparations for and final achievements in baseball.

In a third plot element Mark begins to notice females. He takes a half-conscious romantic interest in a girl his own age, Fortune "Cookie" Rivera, whom he eventually invites to his bar mitzvah because "it was her first chance to see me without my braces. Of course, she never told me how nice I looked without them, but she noticed."[1] Mark does not admit to himself his half-romantic interest in Cookie, but readers see it clearly. In a related plot action, Mark also buys and hides under his mattress a copy of "*Playgirl*" magazine during the course of the story. I take it this also points to Mark's development into male adulthood. (The *Playgirl* of *Bagels* parallels *Playboy*—it contains a centerfold picture of an unclad woman. The actual *Playgirl* magazine—with males as centerfolds—began publication in 1973, four years after *Bagels* was published.)

The fourth plot element is Mark's response to anti-Semitism. One of his teammates, Franklin P. Botts, calls Mark a "Jew Boy" (*BB*, 109). For the remainder of the book Mark struggles with the decision of whether to tell his mother about Botts's outspoken anti-Semitism. The temptation to tell her, and to get Botts thrown off the team, must be great. As Mark tells Herschel later in the story, however, "My telling would be worse than someone else's telling. It wouldn't be right" (*BB*, 140) to use his position as the manager's son for revenge.

Though these four plot elements might seem enough for any one book, Konigsburg adds another: losing, then regaining, a friend. As the story opens Mark's friend Herschel has moved to a more distant neighborhood. Loss of proximity coupled with lack of time have led Herschel and Mark apart, to Mark's sorrow. The book's events, though, lead eventually to the boys' re-establishing their closeness.

Into this small book of 172 pages Konigsburg has woven five plot strands—each element reinforcing the other four. Mark's experience in Little League, his bar mitzvah, his sexual awakening, his ability to pursue the right course concerning Franklin Botts's anti-Semitism, and his ability to renew friendship all converge to help him become a man—or as much of "a man" as any 13-year-old can be.

The Characters

The first thing Mark Setzer tells us about himself is that his mother got "entangled in baseball in . . . [a] way that invaded my privacy and might have declared practically the last little piece of my life as occupied territory" (*BB*, 4–5). Mark is about to become a teenager; privacy is important to him and an important theme of the book. Mark finds his privacy constantly threatened throughout *Bagels*, owing to Bessie's decision to become manager of his baseball team.

Mark's privacy is doubly invaded when his brother Spencer becomes the team's coach. Mark feels the pressure: "When a guy's mother manages and his brother coaches, a guy feels that he loses his right to be awful. A guy feels like he's Exhibit A. Permanent Exhibit A" (*BB*, 62). Thus, though Mark can hit or field with ease away from Bessie and Spencer, "at Little League I was like a watched kettle; I got hot, but I never got up enough steam to boil" (*BB*, 99).

Mark does preserve one area of privacy. He buys a copy of *Playgirl* through an older acquaintance, then hides it. He realizes he could have asked Spencer to buy it for him, but "being that Spencer had too much to do with my life already, I didn't want to ask him" (*BB*, 84). Once he has it and has perused it the first time, he hides the magazine under his mattress in his room. The magazine becomes a focal point for his desire for privacy.

Given that focus, Mark is outraged when he tries to impress Herschel with his having a copy of the magazine only to have an unimpressed "Hersch" tell him that Hersch's new friend, Barry Jacobs, not only keeps his copy of *Playgirl* in view on his desk but has a subscription—a subscription bought for him by his mother. To Mark, this openness "just seems wrong. I don't want my mother looking at my *Playgirl*." Asked, "Why not?," Mark replies, "Because it's mine, that's why" (*BB*, 115). He then replaces his magazine beneath the boxspring, thinking, "I would rather have my one copy that is mine and that I didn't have to share with anyone unless I invited them" (*BB*, 115).

Mark's desire for privacy is probably Konigsburg's chief concern in characterizing him, but several other elements appear. He is unsure of himself, for one thing (like most 12-year-old males). After the first official practice, for example, he asks Spencer, "How did I do?" (*BB*, 58), and is told he seemed afraid of the ball. He asks, "How do you become unafraid?" (*BB*, 59), only to hear from Spencer, "Mostly by becoming more sure of yourself" (*BB*, 59).

Mark's lack of confidence on the field metaphorically represents a myriad of other uncertainties: he is unsure of his ability to chant the haftorah for his upcoming bar mitzvah, to maintain his friendship with Herschel Miller, to confront Franklin Botts's anti-Semitism, and especially to inform his mother and brother that is was cheating which won the championship for the B'nai Bagels.

Like all Jewish males, Mark is to celebrate his bar mitzvah when he becomes 13. He will then become a man—that is, he will from then on be able to take an adult male role in religious ceremonies. The problem is, however, that during the bar mitzvah ceremony each boy must chant a portion of the Torah, and Mark can't chant. His voice is, as he describes it, both "low key [and] off key" (*BB*, 76). Mark asks Spencer's advice. To Mark's amazement, Spencer can help: he tells Mark to chant "*fortissimo*" (*BB*, 82). Though dubious, Mark tries it, and it works—Mark is still hard to listen to but no longer hard to hear. Half his problem has been solved. With that, he loses his uncertainty about the haftorah.

Another major uncertainty in Mark's life concerns his friendship with Hersch. Since Hersch moved to a different neighborhood, he and Mark no longer walk home from school together and haven't time to get together outside such "official" activities as school and Hebrew school. They are drifting apart, especially because Hersch has become a friend to Barry Jacobs, one of the "Crescent Hill Mob" (*BB*, 10). Though Mark, Hersch, and Barry all end up on the B'nai Bagels, Mark finds that he does not fit into the Barry-Hersch relationship.

However badly he wants to win back Hersch's friendship—and however unsure of himself the lost friendship has left him—Mark refuses to take advantage of his position as "manager's son" to discredit Barry in Hersch's eyes. When Mark learns that Barry engineered the cheating that won the championship game, he starts to dial Hersch to tell him Barry's offense. "What would Hersch think of his Crescent Hill buddy now? I picked up the receiver and dialed the first three digits of Hersch's number. But I hung up. . . . I never finished dialing Hersch's number. I never told Hersch about Barry then or ever" (*BB*, 156–57). Mark badly wants to win Hersch back, but he will not be a tattletale to do so.

Resolving another area of uncertainty, Mark also refuses to tattle on teammate Franklin Botts, who calls Mark a "Jew Boy" (*BB*, 109). Botts has already slugged Mark because Mark laughed at him, and Mark has said he won't tell his mother about it. After the "Jew Boy" incident, Mark quietly turns and walks away from Botts and from the ball game they have been playing. Unsure—again—about his own motivation, he still does not tell Bessie about the incident even when he confides it to Hersch and Hersch urges him to tell. Mark grows furious with Hersch at the idea, and Hersch asks, "You sure you're not telling just because you're afraid?" (*BB*, 140). Mark replies, "Of course I'm not sure" (*BB*, 140).

Though Mark is unsure of himself in many areas, his instincts are strong enough to carry him through on difficult decisions. This is apparent when he tells his mother of the cheating which won the Bagels the championship ball game.

When Mark determines that Barry, Botts, and two other team members have cheated to bring about the team's championship win, he mopes for two days, unsure of what to do. He then decides he must tell his mother and brother about the cheating. Though he has the best possible opportunity, and motive, for seeking revenge on the two boys whom he most dislikes, he refuses it. He says instead, "I think you ought to call [the four boys involved in the cheating, including Barry and Botts]. . . . They can give you all the answers. I'm not sure I can" (*BB*, 164).

Mark's handling of the cheating incident resolves his uncertainty. By this time in the book he is a considerably better than average ball player; he feels able to cope with his bar mitzvah; he has regained Hersch's friendship, though they never discuss Barry; and he is able to accept Botts's anti-Semitism as akin to "bad manners" (*BB*, 166). The book's last chapter shows this resolution as Mark reports his successful conclusion of his bar mitzvah. He adds that he has been "becoming"—becoming more himself, his "own kind of tone deaf, center-fielder, son, brother, friend, Bagel" (*BB*, 172). He has found an identity.

As is apparent from the discussion of Mark's characterization, Barry Jacobs is also an important character in *Bagels*. His role is chiefly negative: he is an "anti-Mark," a boy who does not achieve his own identity. Barry lives on Crescent Hill, has his own monthly copy of *Playgirl* ordered for him by his mother, and has no privacy. His lack of privacy, the book suggests, results in his inability to achieve the kind of "becoming" that Mark experiences during the book.

At first, to be sure, the only thing wrong with Barry seems to be that he has displaced Mark as Hersch's best friend. We learn, also, that Barry's mother orders his *Playgirl* for him because, says Hersch, "Mrs. Jacobs doesn't want Barry to hide things from her. She wants to know what he is doing all the time" (*BB*, 114–15).

Soon it becomes clear that Barry plays baseball not as a member of the team but in order to be an individual star: he does not help the other team members improve their skills. Although he is the only boy on the team who can bunt well, he "resented bunting" and "always thought he could get a big hit" (*BB*, 91). Trying to get a big hit, he ignores a signal to bunt in the crucial championship game, and thus fails to move the winning run to scoring position. Barry is about to be responsible for the B'nai Bagels' losing the championship.

Instead, he engineers an illegal switch in pitchers—an illegal switch possible because the Bagels' two pitchers are near-identical twins. With the substitution of the illegal pitcher, the Bagels win the game. As Mark's father later summarizes Barry's character: "Barry doesn't know what flavor Bagel he is. He is his mother's and his father's and his teacher's kind. Nothing but overlapping flavors. It almost wasn't his decision to pull the switch" (*BB*, 166). Spencer adds that it is Barry's lack of privacy which robs him of identity; unlike Mark, he has no identity.

In some ways Bessie is the stereotypical Jewish mother. In arguments with her elder son, Spencer, she gets her feelings "terribly hurt just about every day," which results in "long private discussions with Dad about 'Where have I gone wrong, Sam?'" (*BB*, 4). It is in part because of her unease about Spencer that both her sister and her husband, Sam, urge Bessie to take up "outside interests," which coalesce into managing the B'nai Bagels.

Bessie is not, however, the serious, even neurotic woman the above paragraph might suggest. Her chief characteristic is perhaps best described as suburban Jewish wit. For example, when Spencer first learns that his mother has signed up to manage the B'nai B'rith Little League team, he howls, "Where will you women stop? Why can't you stay in the kitchen?" (*BB*, 15). Shortly thereafter, he suggests that Bessie's mind is closed. Her response: "'My mind is closed? Listen who's talking.' She was conferring with the ceiling again [i.e., looking prayerfully upward]. 'Listen who's talking, will You, dear God? The boy who just said that women should stay in the kitchen thinks that he has an open mind'" (*BB*, 16). Bessie's wit is a constant throughout *Bagels*.

A second element of her characterization appears in this episode. She prays often; she is devout, in fact, though her religious devotion at first appears to be another comical part of her characterization. Bessie spends much of her time in the kitchen and does much of her praying there. Whenever moved to pray she looks upward and addresses the Deity. For Mark, this produces some confusion: "Up until the time I began Sunday School, I thought that [God] lived in the light fixture on our kitchen ceiling" (*BB*, 6).

As the book progresses, Bessie's addresses to the light fixture multiply, and they remain comical. They also appear increasingly devout, in spite of being funny.[2] Thus when her sister Thelma appears at the door just after Bessie has issued a prayerful appeal for help in the upcoming ball game, Bessie "looked up at the kitchen ceiling, and said, So, Casey Stengel she isn't, but she'll do.' She sent a kiss to the Deity by closing her eyes and smacking her lips to the air" (*BB*, 120). God has sent her sister to help her.

Sam later comments that Bessie "is an emotional woman. Whatever she does, she does with her whole heart and soul. And her heart is large, and I think that her soul is, too" (*BB*, 154). The reader will by this point agree that Bessie has both a large heart and a large soul.

Part of that largeness of heart and soul appear in her motivation for taking over the B'nai Bagels. She explains to Thelma, "I want to teach [the team] to care" (*BB*, 73). She wants the boys to care and to win, although winning is not her first priority. As she tells the team prior to their championship game, "I'd say that winning this game would be the second nicest thing in the whole world. The first nicest would be to be able to say that we played hard and honest and up until the very last out" (*BB*, 143). Bessie is sincere when she says "honest"; learning that an illegal pitcher batted, then took the mound in the last inning, she immediately forfeits the championship game.

Funny (or witty), devout, and honest—these attributes almost wholly characterize Bessie Setzer.[3] One further attribute must be added, however: her willingness to leave her children their privacy. Mark feels at the first of the book that she invades his privacy at every turn; later, though, he learns that she has known about his copy of *Playgirl* but has said nothing about it. She has chosen to leave him his privacy. "Thelma, every boy needs to have a little something to hide from his mother," she explains to her sister. "If he finds that he can't have that little corner of privacy at home, he'll look somewhere else for it . . . or [try] to do something really secret and really bad" (*BB*, 132).

Style

Unique among Konigsburg's characters in the earlier books, Bessie retains several Yiddish speech patterns. Early in the book, for example, in an argument with Spencer about stuffed cabbage, she says of adding raisins, "Never. Sauerkraut, I put in my stuffed cabbage. Sauerkraut and a touch of sugar. . . . That makes my mind closed?" (*BB*, 5). The inverted sentence structures are characteristic of a Yiddish dialect, as is Bessie's later use of the endearment "Boychick" (*BB*, 26) to Spencer. Though most of the other characters are also Jewish, only Bessie characteristically uses Yiddish speech patterns.

Konigsburg also regularly uses witty comparisons—perhaps the peak of which appears in Mark's explanation of Little League tournaments. He notes that a team that wins its regional championship gets to play in "a World Series of Little League, and that's a big deal. . . . Little League, Inc., pays your way to Williamsport, Pennsylvania, where the World Series is held. Williamsport, Pennsylvania, is the Jerusalem of Little League" (*BB*, 44).

Konigsburg's third stylistic element—lively, witty dialogue—is characteristic of all her books. Bessie is the prime contributor, as appears after her announcement to Spencer that she has named him coach of the B'nai Bagels. Spencer rebels:

"Mother, I've got school. I've got exams. I've got a social life."

"Yes, Spencer, I hear you. You've also got use of the car. You've also got a generous allowance."

"I need them. How can I commute without them?"

"And I need you, Spencer. How can I manage to manage without you?"

"So what you're telling me is that if I don't coach your team, you are going to take away the car and the allowance."

"Something like that had crossed my mind."

"Aw, Bessie, what the heck kind of psychology is that to raise a son?" Only Spencer didn't say *heck*; he said the other.

Mother answered, "Psychology, it isn't. But it's one heck of a way to get things done." Mother didn't use *heck* either. (*BB*, 25–26)

Konigsburg also creates humorous situations, one of which occurs after Mark has gone to Barry Jacobs's house for dinner. There he observes the family's practice of discussing a stimulating topic—often a current event—during dinner. Mark decides to initiate the practice in his own home:

> The next night at our supper at home I said, "What do you think will happen if the Russians get to the moon first?" My fork fell onto the floor.
> Dad answered, "Please pass the herring."
> I started to pass the dish when it slipped. Only two pieces slid to the floor. . . .
> "Well," I repeated, "What do you think will happen if the Russians get to the moon first?"
> Mother said, "Save some of the potatoes for Spencer; he said that he'd be late home."
> I helped myself to potatoes; they were buttered and parsleyed and only one slipped off the dish. . . . I reached for a roll and knocked over my milk. "Now about the moon," I persisted as I was cupping my hands to catch the dripping and as Mother was running for some paper towels.
> Dad looked up and said, "Mark, why don't you try eating on the floor and see if you can drop things up to the table?" (*BB*, 35–36)

Themes

Konigsburg's central theme in *Bagels,* as with her earlier books, is identity—Mark's achieving identity (and, incidentally, Barry Jacobs's failing to achieve it). Mark's success in this pursuit is attested to by the protagonist himself in the book's last paragraph: "According to Hebrew Law, now I am a man. That is, I can participate fully in all the religious services. But I figure that you don't become a man overnight. Because it is a becoming; becoming more yourself, your own kind of tone deaf, centerfielder, son, brother, friend, Bagel. . . . A lot of it happens being alone" (*BB*, 172).

Friendship is another major theme. Mark's perceived loss of his best friend, Hersch, who had sometimes seemed "more of a brother to [Mark] than Spencer" (*BB*, 10), is a loss he feels keenly. Hersch is different enough from Mark that the two "file down each other's rough edges" (*BB*, 10). Throughout the book Mark misses Hersch, and misses, almost in the abstract, their friendship. As he says, "It was like one and one making two, and two is a good number to face the world with. As a matter of fact, I think that's the reason so many people get married, and as a matter of fact, I think that's the reason I wanted to get Hersch back" (*BB*, 87). The two eventually re-establish their friendship, though there is still "that small part about Barry" (*BB*, 169) which they do not discuss; their friendship is not what it was, but it is "pretty good" (*BB*, 169).

The final means whereby Konigsburg shows Mark gaining his identity involves his learning to care about his ball team. Early in *Bagels* Mark notes that his membership on last year's B'nai B'rith team had been "pretty depressing" (*BB*, 19), as they lost most of their games by one-sided scores. The season was even worse than depressing, Mark decides; it was boring.

Bessie decides the team must learn to care—and she gets the results she wanted. The B'nai Bagels win their first, second, and third games:

> And then we lost our fourth game to the Elks, and we felt rotten. Mother had wanted that, too. She and Spencer analyzed and scolded and made us work harder, and we won again.
> She had made the team care, and she (and Spencer) had given us enough training to make it count. (*BB*, 96)

"Caring," though, is not synonymous with winning. Bessie's first priority is to play both "hard and honest" (*BB*, 143). After Bessie has learned of the cheating and forfeited the game, she turns to her husband and asks, "Did I make them care too much, Sam?" (*BB*, 166). (The reader may be asking the same question at this point.) Sam replies, "No, Bessie. . . . The trouble didn't come about because the team cared too much. The trouble came because Barry couldn't stand being wrong and being a loser" (*BB*, 166). The point seems to be that caring makes you want to win, but it doesn't make you want to cheat.

Mark Setzer becomes a man at his bar mitzvah. *About the B'nai Bagels* (New York: Atheneum, 1969), 171.

Comparable Fiction

Bagels might at first seem a "sports story," that much-maligned subcategory of children's literature. It concerns Little League baseball, to be sure, but it does not resemble the formula sports story. (Compare the books of John R. Tunis, some of the best in the field. "Small-town boy makes good" is an oversimplification of Tunis's sports stories, but not by much.) *Bagels* does not contain sustained playing sequences, as do most sports stories; instead, it focuses on the life of Mark Setzer, whose personal concerns are more important than baseball. In *Bagels* baseball becomes a metaphor for growing up.

Bruce Brooks's *The Moves Make the Man* (1984) makes an interesting comparison-contrast here. *Moves* contains extended basketball-playing sequences, and basketball is central in a way that baseball is not central to *Bagels*. At the same time, the books have several elements in common: basketball is a metaphor in *Moves* just as baseball is in *Bagels,* and *Moves* is very much about boys becoming men, just as *Bagels* is. The racial issue in *Moves* also parallels the anti-Semitic issue in *Bagels,* but it is considerably more of an issue, and more frightening, than in *Bagels*. Jerome, the 13-year-old black narrator, is barred from playing on his new school's basketball team even though he fulfills the coach's conditions; his race alone prevents his making the team. Later, the owner of a café refuses to serve him and calls his white friend a "nigger lover" and Jerome a "jigaboo" as he evicts them.[4]

(George)

Like Mark Setzer, Benjamin Carr finds his identity in the course of *(George)*. Unlike Mark, however, Ben does not seek growth; he tries to avoid it. But the little man inside him prevails.

The Plot

Set in "Lawton Beach," Florida—a cross between Miami Beach and Fort Lauderdale—*(George)* concerns Benjamin Dickinson Carr; his little brother, Howard McHune Carr; and "George,"

Ben's "concentric twin,"[5] as the narrator puts it. George is a little man who has always lived inside Ben. The story opens two
years before the present action and is narrated in the third person—two new techniques for Konigsburg.

As the story begins, the Ben of two years past is entering
sixth grade. Because Ben is an exceptionally bright student, he
is also entering an organic chemistry class along with older students in "Astra," a public school for gifted children. Another
member of the organic chemistry class, twelfth-grader William
Hazlitt, has in prior years profited from inviting the science ace
Ben to be his lab partner. Only seniors are permitted to do research in a new program just beginning its trial run at Astra;
thus William may do research and Ben may not—nor can he be
William's lab partner.

William and his new partner, Cheryl, choose to do research
secretly on LSD, which they intend to sell to the annually appearing horde of college students, thus making money but also
buying their way into the college set. Ben discovers this and
determines to upset their plans. He does so, but has to take the
blame for manufacturing their LSD. He sacrifices his reputation
in order to save the research program and Mr. Berkowitz, the
chemistry teacher. William and Cheryl do not escape the conse-
quences, however; when Ben later tells Mr. Berkowitz the truth,
he flunks the two seniors, who, the narrator hopes, may learn
something from the experience.

The Characters

Charlotte Carr, the mother of Ben and Howard (and also
claimed as mother by George), figures prominently in *(George)*.
So does Mr. Berkowitz, the Astra chemistry teacher, and Marilyn Carr, the two children's stepmother (their parents have divorced about four years before the action of the story). The main
characters, though, are the youths: William Hazlitt, Howard,
Ben, and George.

Being a phony, William is the closest thing in Konigsburg's
works to a repeating character—he is similar to Cynthia
(Jennifer) and to Barry Jacobs *(Bagels)*. William strives to be
different from everyone else, or at least to appear different. At a
school where everyone was allowed to be different, William

found it hard to be unique, but he managed: "At Astra where everyone wore sport shirts and casual clothes, sometimes even Bermuda shorts, William took to wearing a suit and vest and tie" (*G*, 26). Though William works so hard to be unique, his differences from others prove superficial. In the crucial area of identity, William is a blank. As George says of William and Cheryl's trying to "buy their way into . . . the college crowd," "They have no identity, . . . so they work hard at being different from their group. They don't realize they're just trying to fit into another group. The crowd may be different, but they're not" (*G*, 133).

Ben's younger brother, Howard, plays a secondary role in *(George)*, but Konigsburg characterizes him sharply. His major characteristic, at least as observed by adults, is his grouchiness, which evidently appeared shortly after birth: "When . . . Howard . . . was still an infant, he had cried a lot and his problem was called *colic*. As he got older, it was hard to know what to call it; but whatever it was, it couldn't be called an improvement. He didn't cry anymore; he grouched. George explained that Howard never really learned to talk; he just learned to talk back" (*G*, 4). The character of Howard, whose two "particular talents" the narrator lists as "common sense and bad manners" (*G*, 15), is consistent throughout *(George)*.

Though conspicuously lacking in manners, Howard has acquired another useful skill: intensive observation of a school-bus driver has taught him how to drive a car. Toward the close of *(George)* Benjamin must get to the Astra chemistry lab and steal William and Cheryl's LSD before they can sell it to the college students. Without Howard's driving skills he could neither get there on time nor carry off all the suspect material.

Howard does not perform in *(George)* merely as an exemplar of bad manners and driving skills, however. He is also an example of how lovable a sibling—even a grouchy one—can be: "Even when Howard was merely an infantile civil disorder, George was discovering nice things about him and telling Ben about them. . . . 'Look,' he would say to make certain that Ben noticed that Howard had told his best friend, Raymond, that yellow was the best color because his big brother Ben had said so" (*G*, 10). Howard also copies Ben's habit of eating ketchup on his soft-boiled eggs, and he imitates Ben's wave. As a result, "Ben learned to love him. Impossible Howard. Impossible him" (*G*, 11).

William Hazlitt and Howard Carr are important characters, but Ben and his concentric twin George make up the main character interest in *(George)*. With Ben, David Rees has remarked, Konigsburg seems to have produced "another psychological study [of] another neurotic . . . child" (Rees, 81). John Rowe Townsend has even worried that George, "the cause of . . . psychiatric treatment" that Ben receives during the course of the story, is a sign of Ben's "deeply ambiguous mental state," which may confuse, even trouble, some children (Townsend, 119). Clearly, there is room for confusion concerning the relationship of Ben and George. The confusion appears in the novel, too; various adults are perplexed, troubled, or outright alarmed when Ben inadvertently betrays George's existence.

One cannot safely conjecture how all child readers may react to George; "delight," Rees's term, has been a common response. The children in the book have no difficulties with George: both Ben and Howard accept George and enjoy him. Before Howard's birth Ben had mentioned George to his mother, who simply assumed George to be an "imaginary playmate" of the sort many "creative children" fashion for themselves (*G*, 3–4). She expects this imaginary playmate to disappear on Howard's birth, and Ben accommodatingly allows George to disappear on schedule, "altogether inside" (*G*, 4). This only means, however, that Ben no longer mentions George to his mother; George and Ben still hold conversations—conversations into which Howard comes to be included when he reaches kindergarten. George chooses to speak to Howard in a "special deep voice" (*G*, 14), and Howard simply accepts George as a kindred spirit—that is, George is unmannerly (in speech) and cynical; Howard gets along well with him.

Ben and George differ sharply in characterization. Though an outstanding student with precocious proficiency in science, Ben appears in most of *(George)* as a conformist. He seeks acceptance almost frantically—from William, from Mr. Berkowitz, from the world in general. George, on the other hand, seeks individuality. He does not seek William's shop-worn substitutes for

The visible half of Benjamin Dickinson Carr entering his classroom.
(George) (New York: Atheneum, 1970), 19.

individuality but genuine individuality, which he desires for Ben.

Ben's special abilities are from the first linked to George. As a kindergartner Ben had memorized a poem about a starfish after going over it with his mother. He not only repeats the poem to her but, prompted by George, goes on to explain "how the starfish used suction to walk and to open clams" (*G*, 6). Mrs. Carr is duly impressed, and soon after she and Ben's father enroll Ben in Astra, where he and George have a grand time in science courses: "Ben and George had taken biology when Ben was in the fourth grade. . . . George had enjoyed [it] enormously. . . . He had memorized the names of all the bones for Ben and the names of all the plant phyla . . . and he had helped Ben to spell everything correctly" (*G*, 8). George is not, however, a mere supermemory: "George was best at solving problems that required a new way of looking at things. Sometimes it would be a zany word that George would say or sometimes just a wild point of view" (*G*, 9; and see 114).

George is wildness, the necessary touch of the uninhibited. Though he does not like organic chemistry (because of the way Ben approaches it), he is not opposed to knowledge. Rather, he feels that "people ought to enjoy the pursuit of knowing as well as the knowing" (*G*, 24). His quarrel with Ben's approach is that Ben "was galloping into the field of science, straight for the stable, not allowing George to smell the flowers along the way" (*G*, 24). George likes curiosity and insight; he scorns an approach about which he can say, "All the answers are in books anyway" (*G*, 39). Ben does not understand George's point here. "Of course they're in books" (*G*, 39), he rejoins. Konigsburg clearly deplores Ben's leaning toward mere cookbook chemistry.

George deplores it too. His nature, even his function, is to keep Ben from hiding "inside a test tube" (*G*, 92), as he puts it. In their final dialogue George tells Ben to "listen to me always . . . especially now, as the pull of your courses and the pull of your classmates tries to drown out my voice forever. It's a critical time, Ben. Always listen to me, Ben. If you don't shut me up forever now, I'll be rich within you" (*G*, 149).

George begins to sound very sober indeed. Not so, however; as the book's first sentence points out, George is "the funniest little man in the whole world" (*G*, 3). His humor often appears in the form of sarcasm, as when he comments on Ben's mother's cooking: "Please tell the Queen of the Maytag that the oven will not roast the turkey unless it happens to be turned on. . . . I swear that if that lady, our mother, had a General Electric oven, it would get broken to corporal" (*G*, 30, 41). This antimother sarcasm is all in-house, however; when anyone beyond the Ben-George-Howard circle seeks to criticize Charlotte Carr, George leaps to her defense.

Aside from his wild points of view and his humor, George is a completely honest character. He always tells the truth, often with brutal directness. He heartily disapproves of Ben's allowing William to use Ben's lab results, and thus to cheat, and he hates phonies—which explains his dislike of William.

Ben, as distinct from George, doesn't have wild points of view. In fact, during *(George)* he comes close to losing any point of view beyond the norm. He actively seeks the norm, almost to the point of losing George.

Ben's desire to be normal—to be accepted—was not a problem in earlier years, when, as the narrator reports, he "never avoided other students; he just didn't make time for them" (*G*, 8). Instead, he did science and other school work, coped with home responsibilities, and talked with George. Those activities filled his days. He thinks of himself as "born special" (*G*, 15, 9), and George is all the company he needs.

As *(George)* opens, however, that situation has changed. George is no longer company enough for Ben, who rushes to get to his new organic chemistry class in time to get a seat with William and is crestfallen when a seating list and his nonsenior status separate him from his hero. George does not like William; Ben idolizes him. At one point Ben even "grovels" (as George puts it) in an attempt to ingratiate himself with William. It is Ben's idolizing William that leads him to give William some purified benzene from his successful lab exercise. William and Cheryl had spilled their benzene and failed to do the exercise properly; thus Ben helps them cheat.

Ben also grovels to his chemistry teacher, Mr. Berkowitz. When Ben and his family meet Mr. Berkowitz on the beach, Ben tries to "make an impression" (*G*, 49), asking about the senior research program and mentioning William as a "sort of" (G, 48–49) good friend. "Ben thought he had to advertise to sell his friendship" (G, 49), George concludes about this incident.

Groveling to Mr. Berkowitz does Ben little harm, though George finds it unattractive. Ben's frantic desire to win William's friendship, though, is unhealthy. It leads him to help William cheat, and it leads him to demean himself in conversations with William. George points all this out to Ben, who doesn't want to hear anything against William or against his pursuit of William's friendship. Driven to anger, Ben finally says to his inner voice, "Oh, shut up, George! Shut up already!" (G, 93). To Ben's growing dismay, George shuts up—and stays silent for weeks.

George's silence proves particularly troubling to Ben, because just as George decides to shut up, Ben is diagnosed as a "paranoid schizophrenic" by his stepmother, a home economics major who minored in psychology. She and Ben's father have overheard a late-night discussion between Ben and George—the latter of whom, in a departure from his usual custom, had spoken out loud. She and Ben's father send Ben to a psychiatrist, to whom George refuses to talk. The psychiatrist decides George is a projection of Ben's darker desires. Ben, fully aware of the adult furor he has occasioned, keeps quiet and tries to ride out the storm. He feels very much bullied by the adult world, however, and puzzled by William and Cheryl's odd chemistry project. He wants George to help him figure it out. He needs George, in fact; this is "a situation that was more than its parts" (G, 123), and analyzing such situations is George's specialty.

George refuses to reappear, however, and Ben is left to his own devices. Trying to analyze the strange behavior of the two seniors, he fulfills an earlier promise to George and looks up some information about the project William and Cheryl are pursuing. At that point, several earlier observations fall into place and Ben realizes the two seniors are planning to manufacture LSD. Acting on his own, he mobilizes Howard to oversee the driving and heads for the school laboratory to frustrate the LSD plan. Ben has finally awakened to the difference between surface and substance; he no longer idolizes William.

At this point George reappears, and helps Ben think out how

to avoid getting Mr. Berkowitz's senior research program into trouble. With George's help, Ben resolves the messy situation with considerable fairness. He does incur a damaged reputation in the process. As he points out to George, however, the stigma will not last, and it will not act against Astra.

Overall, *(George)* is Ben's book; it is the story of his almost involuntarily seeking, and finding, his own identity. In characterizing Ben, Konigsburg has shown a precocious boy whose emotional growth has not kept up with his intellectual abilities. During the action of the book Ben's "concentric twin" helps him grow to responsible maturity ("maturity" defined as 10- to 12-year-old caring for others and behaving responsibly). Ben does not grow beyond George; in a sense, he absorbs George. By the last page of the story, "Ben's . . . voice had deepened . . . [and] had become indistinguishable from George's" (*G*, 152). Ben has achieved integrity—wholeness.

Style

(George) is Konigsburg's first books to use an omniscient third-person narrator. Interestingly, Konigsburg's narrator uses many more sentence fragments than appeared in the earlier books. In addition, her metaphors are fresh evidence of her originality as a stylist; as in the earlier books, moreover, her wittiness appears at several points.

The third-person narrator's use of sentence fragments, or elliptical sentences, adds to *(George)* a wholly different tone. A few fragments do appear in the characters' dialogue, as was sporadically the case in Konigsburg's earlier works. To the narrator, however, are reserved roughly 40 separate fragments in 152 pages. These fragments add a staccato underline to the material, like a spondee in a line of iambs, as in these examples:

> "[Except for Ben, Howard] was the only other person that George had ever spoken out loud to. *For a long time.*" (*G*, 3; my italics)

> [On an LSD trip, Cheryl's] eyes looked like the punched-out holes in two-ring notebook paper. *Dark and strangely unblinking.* She looked as if she were cooking on the inside with something that was pulling all the moisture from her skin. *Bright but powdery.* (*G*, 115; my italics)

Konigsburg's metaphors are another stylistic element in *(George)*. Some are quick comparisons, as when she describes Mr. Berkowitz's smile: "His teeth looked like a row of Chiclets beneath his moustache" *(G*, 59). Other metaphors extend from a few lines to several pages, like the longer metaphor that compares Ben's increasing specialization with his approach to building sand castles: "Ben started another turret, and Howard moved over to trim the one that Ben had just completed. . . . Ben was . . . building more towers and building them faster and faster and never taking time to look at the whole thing. He was doing that with his life, too. And George's" *(G*, 52; the metaphor continues to the next page).

A minor element in *(George)* that young readers probably find humorous is the "foul language" mentioned in the book's first sentence. George does use what children often see as foul language: he says "damn" several times, he calls Ben's stepmother a "jackass" *(G*, 86), and, in persuading Howard to attend a private kindergarten called "The Wee House in the Woods," he doubles "just one word in the school's name" *(G*, 13–14), which makes it sound ridiculous enough that Howard is willing to try the school a month at a time.

Konigsburg in *(George)* also ventures into the mildly bawdy humor that is to recur in her books: when kindergartner Ben discusses with his mother a starfish's anatomy, "he said something for tentacles that made Mrs. Carr laugh out loud" *(G*, 6–7).

Themes

Konigsburg's theme of identity appears again in *(George)*. Ben is establishing his identity. At first, he seems to be doing poorly: he tries to impress Mr. Berkowitz (and others) because he "doesn't understand friendship" *(G*, 49) and because he is not comfortable with himself. As the narrator puts it, "Ben felt uneasy [after trying to impress Mr. Berkowitz], not quite knowing why, but knowing that the feeling was familiar and happening often lately. . . . Ben had wanted to impress Mr. Berkowitz, and he wasn't sure if he had succeeded" *(G*, 51).

That lack of self-assurance extends to Ben's relationship with his father. Whenever Ben visits his father and stepmother in Norfolk, Virginia, "he always had the feeling of wanting to be at his tiptoe best" (*G*, 72), because he wants to be a "truly terrific fellow" for his father. The results are not pleasant: "The days before a visit to his father were filled with fantasies about how he would look to his dad, and the days following were filled with wondering if he had been a success" (*G*, 73). In short, as *(George)* opens Ben equates "success" with "impress" in his relationships with others. He is not comfortable in—does not feel he has—an identity of his own.

Thus Ben seeks a role model. His chief candidate is William, which could have proven disastrous. As it happens, his own good sense—that is, his own George—persuades him that William is no model. George early on concludes, then maintains throughout, that William has sacrificed "curiosity and insight . . . for appearances and the conquest of success" (*G*, 24), that his identity is only superficial. Ben, however—using his own common sense and assisted by his little man inside—achieves his own personhood. He takes the blame for manufacturing the LSD so the science program at Astra can continue, but he arranges for Cheryl and William to receive significant punishment nonetheless. Moreover—and this leads to a third theme—he follows George's lead in changing his approach toward learning and knowing.

The major theme in *(George)* is surely Konigsburg's examination of how one thinks, or how one knows. She might almost have been reading the work of William G. Perry, whose classic study points out that thinking can develop from dualistic "black and white" approaches to multiplistic "black-gray-white" (or *no* blacks and whites) thinking. It can also stop dead at a dualistic, simplistic view of knowing.[6]

Ben's approach to learning has become a "black-or-white" one in the early pages of *(George)*. He feels that all the answers "are in books" (*G*, 39), an approach that precludes having insights or generating new knowledge. He has become so involved in memorizing and in cookbook chemistry that George often "had to fight to get Ben to put his head back and listen as they reviewed [a] problem together" (*G*, 24). Ben is resisting thinking. Instead of enjoying the "pursuit of knowing" (*G*, 24; i.e., thinking), Ben gallops "into the field of science, straight for the stable" (*G*, 24), as George sees it. George sees him as about to become "*merely* a chemist"—that is, "a neat, prepackaged chemist who fits things into neat, labeled jars" (*G*, 77–78). George is the antithesis of this sort of prefabricated knowing; he likes "curiosity and insight" (*G*, 24), qualities that do not come prefabricated, and specializes in "a wild point of view" (*G*, 9).

In contrasting the two phonies, William and Cheryl, with the clearly authoritative George—and in her sympathetic portrayal of the developing Ben—Konigsburg makes a clear statement in favor of intellectual flexibility as a way fully to realize one's identity.

A final theme—one personally relevant to many of Konigsburg's readers—is that of divorce. Konigsburg shows the effects of divorce both on children and on a parent (here Charlotte Carr alone; Ben's father never appears in the book). The effects on Charlotte Carr receive sympathetic mention. First, Howard and Ben never think of how she feels when every Christmas they go to spend the holidays at their father's home, and she never tells them. Each time, though, "she hugged them special . . . as she put them on the plane" (*G*, 74). A second effect of divorce for Charlotte Carr appears in her fear that Ben's supposed mental illness will show that she is not a good mother. Then, she fears, the court will remove Ben from her care and require that he live with Mr. Carr and his new wife.

Divorce is not easy for Charlotte Carr; the effect on the two children, though, receives more attention. Once, trying to list "the advantages of having divorced parents" (*G*, 74), they immediately put having two yearly Christmases on the list, but can find nothing else. They visit their father "during Christmas, during Easter, and for one month during the summer, but they didn't much care for it. It was in the contract under visiting privileges" (*G*, 71). The lackluster tone reflects their feeling about the visits; the boys are contracted for like commodities.

Unlike commodities, though, they can worry about their position. Thus before each visit Ben worries about impressing his father favorably; afterwards he worries about whether he was successful. Why? "Ben was nagged by the suspicion that if he had been a truly terrific fellow, his father would never have left" (*G*, 73). One of divorce's major pressures on children appears in that thought.

Konigsburg does not hesitate to write significant themes into her works, as she had done in her three earlier books. In *(George)* she again deals with identity, but she adds the issues of learning and divorce. Embodying these themes in a book that comes across as light, funny, and witty is no mean feat.

Comparable Fiction

As is often the case with Konigsburg's books, *(George)* does not directly compare with any other children's book. Some of the standard reference works have discussed it as dealing "with a serious problem, the schizoid personality."[7] One need only, however, compare such works as William Mayne's *Gideon Ahoy* (1989) and Betsy Byars's *The Summer of the Swans* (1970) to realize that *(George)* does not concern mental illness at all—there is nothing of slowness, malperception, or misperception about George himself, or about the Ben-George combination. Neither is there the sense of loss that pervades, for example, *The Summer of the Swans*, whose 10-year-old Charlie "hasn't spoken a word since he was three years old, . . . since his illness," and who suffers "great parts of his life that were lost to [him], blank spaces that he could never fill in."[8]

Though *(George)* is unique, the closeness between Ben and Howard compares with other children's books that discuss loving sibling relationships. Cynthia Voigt's Tillerman family series (*Homecoming*, *Dicey's Song*, etc.), Margaret Mahy's *The Haunting* (1983), and Virginia Hamilton's *Sweet Whispers, Brother Rush* (1982) come to mind as books where siblings may quarrel but remain firmly aware of their love for one another.

(George) also shares the theme of divorce with other modern children's books. Both Judy Blume's *It's Not the End of the World* (1972) and Vera and Bill Cleaver's *Ellen Grae* (1967) deal with divorce; each suggests that children of divorced parents can cope and even prevail.

In *(George)* Ben and Howard clearly dislike their parents' being divorced, but equally clearly they can cope with the situation. Their father does not figure in the book beyond bare mention; their mother, though, provides a great deal of loving attention. Her fear of being thought not a good mother will be familiar to many single parents, and to many child readers.

Conclusion

Bagels and *(George)* differ from Konigsburg's earlier books in presenting male protagonists and an increased adult presence. Both continue to explore identity, and each has a unique plot. *(George)* is much the more complex of the two. We quickly see George, Ben's "concentric twin," as the most fascinating part of the book that bears his name. Ben has more lines, but George's are funnier. Ben's characterization is stronger, too, because we see him work out his own identity during the course of the book. (As the book opens George has already formed his identity and does not change.) Nonetheless, George deserves his star billing. The book's first sentence names him, and its last paragraph tells us that "for all the rest of his life, Ben will be mindful of his inner parts. He'll . . . never swallow orange seeds or watermelon pits because to do so could bring on an attack of appendicitis, and that he realizes would involve surgery" (*G*, 152). Then Konigsburg's last illustration appears. Ben and Howard are striding along the street, with their shadows stretched out beside them. A much smaller shadow—with no visible body—strides along between them. (George.)

Precisely what George is in this book is an interesting question. Ben's mother would say he was Ben's imaginary childhood playmate who reappeared at a stressful time in Ben's life. Howard would simply say he is a little man who lives inside Ben. Ben's stepmother would say he is a phenomenon of Ben's paranoid schizophrenia. Ben's psychiatrist would characterize him as a delusion, a projection of Ben's darker desires of which he is eventually able to cure Ben. (Most of Ben's world would agree with the psychiatrist.)

The reader is left intriguingly unsure. At first we wonder if George is simply that imaginary childhood companion retained to an unusually late age. Then we wonder if Ben's stepmother, or perhaps the psychiatrist, might be on the right track. Then, seeing the good outcomes of George's suggestions, some readers will see George as a projection—either Ben's or Konigsburg's—of precocious mental ability. After all, George helps Ben remember things like atomic weights, names of plant phyla, and so forth. More important, the narrator points out, is George's off-center viewpoint, which enables Ben to view problems creatively. No cookbook chemistry (or biology—or physics) for George. Is he, then, a metaphor for creativity? For precocity?

Konigsburg leaves the question unresolved. That last illustration is her last teasing question: Is George "real" or a projection? The best part of the book is Konigsburg's refusal to answer that question; this is something we must decide individually. Most child readers will accept George as "real" on their first reading; later readings may produce other interpretations.

4

The Short Stories

Altogether, One at a Time

Asked by an interviewer in 1986, "Which one of your books are you the most satisfied with . . . ?," Konigsburg replied, "The short stories come the closest" (Jones interview, 179). We can understand this response. These stories' consistently witty style, coupled with their interesting characterization and profound themes, make them both enjoyable and memorable. We see in *Altogether, One at a Time* (1971) an interest in the interaction of text and illustration that will eventually fructify in Konigsburg's later picture books. *Altogether, One at a Time* consists of four short stories, each illustrated by a different artist.

"Inviting Jason"
(illustrated by Mercer Mayer)

"Inviting Jason" is narrated by Stanley. He is just turning 10, and the story opens as he sends out six birthday-party invitations. He does not invite Jason. His mother orders, "Invite him,"[1] so Stanley obeys—but not willingly. He does not care for Jason. Jason has dyslexia, and Stanley feels that this sort of difference bars Jason from polite company.

Stanley prefers Dick, the first boy he invites to his party: "Dick was the fastest runner in the fourth grade and the second fastest in the whole school" (*A*, 4), and Stanley wants to win his friendship. To his dismay, however, Dick and Jason interact cordially during the party. Dick even admires Jason's uncommon writing and drawing, though Stanley feels the efforts of the dyslexic boy are "spooky," certainly unlike those of the other boys and therefore wrong. Dick, however, praises Jason's work, talks to Jason at some length, and says "three more nice things about Jason" (*A*, 12) after Jason has left Stanley's home.

Stanley does not echo Dick's sentiments. Instead, when at the close of the story his mother asks him, "Aren't you glad that you asked Jason, after all?" Stanley responds, "No!" As the above quotation shows, he suffers no charitable afterthoughts about Jason. He wishes Jason had not come to the party; Dick likes him too much.

Konigsburg's characterization is not a matter of black and white. Jason is not perfect. For example, he accidentally spits on the birthday cake. But Dick, the popular runner, can see that Jason's difference—his dyslexia—makes him interesting. His writing about astronauts, and his drawing of the astronauts on the moon, seem to Dick interesting and appropriate to their unearthly topic. The reader will probably agree with Dick, and realize that Stanley is mean-spirited.

"Mean-spirited," on second thought, is too strong. Stanley is what most 10-year-olds (and many adults) are: intolerant of difference. His intolerance is Konigsburg's chief theme in this story: she shows that Stanley can embrace differences of the "fastest runner" sort, but not dyslexia; he almost speaks of it as a disease. We are likely to view Stanley negatively, then come to realize he is simply a standard young boy, perhaps a little more insensitive than usual. The realization might cause other youths to re-examine their own prejudices.

Five illustrations appear in the story. They are pleasant, but the text does not rely on them—that is, the text would still make sense without them (which is not the case for the collection's other stories and their illustrations).

Perhaps the most interesting element of "Inviting Jason" appears in the coupling of Stanley's unrelievedly negative attitude toward Jason with the positive attitude the reader comes to feel toward him. This results both from Dick's approval and from the obvious meanness of Stanley's motives and responses. Feeling Jason is the underdog, the reader sympathizes with him. A similar treatment of a learning-disabled child appears in Cynthia Voigt's Tillerman-family series; Maybeth, the younger girl, is a slow learner—even thought to be retarded by a succession of teachers (see *Homecoming* and *Dicey's Song*). The situation differs, though; the external world considers Maybeth retarded, while her family stoutly (and rightly) maintains that she is just "slow,"[2] and—as James demonstrates in *Dicey's Song*—that she can learn if material is presented in a way she can grasp.

In all three works, the reader not only sympathizes with the learning-disabled child but reads that the child has compensating gifts: Jason, says Dick, writes and illustrates interestingly about astronauts. Maybeth, similarly, has a gift for music; she sings and plays piano with genius.

"The Night of the Leonids"
(illustrated by Laurel Schindelman)

Ten-year-old Lewis narrates this story. His parents being on one of their frequent trips abroad, he is visiting his grandmother. On his first evening at her New York apartment, the two play cards, then she reads the newspaper. She finds an article about the Commissioner of Parks inviting "everyone to Central Park tonight" (A, 19) to see "a shower of stars" (A, 20). A meteor shower is about to take place; falling stars ("the Leonids") from a comet's tail will appear in the sky over Central Park just that one night, and then not again for 33 years.

Lewis and his grandmother decide they should go see the "upside-down Grand Canyon of fireworks" (A, 23) the star shower will be. Each is eager to view the spectacle. "Why didn't you see it [last time when you were 30]?" asks Lewis. "I lost my chance," says his grandmother. Lewis says no more, musing, "I knew about lost chances" (A, 25).

The two go to Central Park around midnight and wait for the shower to begin. Instead, clouds roll in and cover the sky. Lewis cries, saying "I'll be forty-three before I can ever see a Leonid." His grandmother greets the comment with "Oh, shut up!" When Lewis adds, "I'll be *middle-aged*" (A, 27), his grandmother whacks him on the bottom.

"What did I do?" asks the perplexed—and hurt—Lewis.

"'You add it up,' Grandmother said. Not kindly" (A, 28). He adds his grandmother's present age of 63 years to the 33 years until the Leonids again appear, and realizes they "don't add up to another chance." He says nothing. They walk back to her apartment holding hands, though they do not usually hold hands. Lewis confides in the last sentence of the story, "I held the hand that hit me" (A, 28).

Konigsburg characterizes Lewis as a smart aleck but sensitive. Thus he greets the headline, "Commissioner of Parks invites everyone to Central Park tonight" with "What for? . . . A mass mugging?" (A, 19). His sensitivity appears early as he says, "Grandmother likes to be listened to. That's one reason why she explains things. . . . When she *explains*, I listen. I sit close and listen close, and that makes her feel like a regular grandmother. She likes that, and sometimes so do I. That's one reason why we get along pretty well" (A, 21). A recurring comment in this story, in fact, is "we get along pretty well, Grandmother and I" (A, 15; repeated in variants on 18, 21, and 27).

Lewis's sensitivity to and fondness for his grandmother allows him to understand why she spanks him when he cries at missing the Leonids. As Lewis has already said, he knows "about lost chances" (A, 25); he seems also to sense the chill his grandmother feels at the thought that her years are drawing to a close, as this "lost chance" points out. Konigsburg characterizes him overall as moving from the Stanley sort of self-centeredness to his understanding of, and sympathy for, his grandmother's situation.

As always with Konigsburg, humor and wit characterize her style. Lewis's wisecracks appear on every page; moreover, any child, or any adult, will recognize and smile at the teasing rivalry that occurs after Grandmother has announced that "Something special" (A, 19) will take place in Central Park:

I waited for what was a good pause before I asked, "What special?"

Grandmother waited for a good pause before she answered, "Something spectacular," not even bothering to look up from the newspaper.

I paused. Grandmother paused. I paused. Grandmother paused. I paused, I paused, I paused, and I won. Grandmother spoke first. "A spectacular show of stars," she said. (*A*, 19–20)

Child readers will enjoy seeing Lewis win this exchange.

Konigsburg and her illustrators begin in this story, and continue in "Camp Fat" and in "Momma at the Pearly Gates," to make text and illustrations mutually dependent. The best example is perhaps the half-page picture of clouds covering the sky. The illustration follows the lines, "We waited. And waited. And saw." *What* they saw never appears in the text; only from the illustration does one know that clouds have obscured the star shower.

The relationship of old and young—a new theme for Konigsburg—is of major interest here. The camaraderie Lewis and his grandmother experience rings true in the story. Like other stories about friendly grandparent-grandchild relationships—for instance, Barbara Williams's *Kevin's Grandma* (1975), which features another unconventional grandmother, and Mavis Jukes's *Blackberries in the Dark* (1985), which also addresses mortality, in this case the recent death of the grandfather, bringing grandson and grandmother together to console each other—this story seems written for the younger end of the 8-to-14 spectrum. Another Konigsburg short story about old-young relationships is "At the Home," discussed below.

"Camp Fat"
(illustrated by Gary Parker)

This story's focus is apparent from its title. Clara, the narrator, has been sent to Camp Fat (Camp To Ke Ro No) because she is fat. In fact, all we know about Clara is that she is "a kid" (*A*, 32) and fat. Konigsburg inserts "fat" in the story's first sentence, then repeats it nine times in two pages. Clara's parents hope she will lose most or all of her fat at the camp, which specializes in thinning its campers. She will be at the camp for six weeks, and her "goal" is to lose 15 pounds.

Early in her camp experience Clara meets Miss Natasha, a counselor. Miss Natasha interacts with the campers only at night—Friday night for Clara's cabin. Miss Natasha's purpose as counselor is to "have dialogue" with selected campers. Following her first dialogue with Clara, Miss Natasha pats Clara's knee and a ring on Miss Natasha's little finger, "a plain looking gold dome ring" (A, 34), springs open. Inside it is a tiny watch that Clara finds "most beautiful" (A, 34). It has a mother-of-pearl face with some numbers replaced by jeweled flowers: "The hands seemed to float to the proper time. . . . I thought that that was just a plain old ring'" (A, 36), Clara exclaims.

Miss Natasha's second visit features a hard-to-open locket. On her third call she shows Clara "the ugliest, smelliest looking blob that I had ever seen" (A, 45). She explains to Clara that when she was allowed to leave her country (Russia, one assumes) she was only let bring one item with her. She encased the item in plastic, which she now knows was a mistake: "I should have known better than to think that adding layers of plastic could preserve all of my fine workmanship. A plain, simple but strong exterior would have been better." She suggests to Clara that she peel the plastic away "a little bit at a time" (A, 45) because "it's worth it" (A, 46) to see what's inside.

Clara at first rejects the idea, saying it would be too much work "just to get a look" (A, 46). Miss Natasha rejoins, "That's what you expect of everyone you meet. . . . You expect everyone to see what is inside all that fat of yours. And not everyone can take the time" (A, 47). Clara rejects the task nonetheless; Miss Natasha leaves the cabin. She returns in a week, and after some urging Clara accepts the blob and starts peeling off layers of smelly plastic.

In another week or two Clara has peeled off enough plastic to see that something "gold and the size of an airmail stamp" (A, 51) is inside. On the last Friday of her camp experience Clara finishes the peeling in Miss Natasha's presence. She finds a tiny gold book with a jeweled cover. She opens it to discover a poem and a picture. The short poem reads: "Oh, my pretty, / Oh, my Clara / Oh, my pretty, / Oh, my love" (A, 51–55), at one line per page. On the fifth page appears the picture—a picture of a little girl, Clara, not fat. Clara cries, "Oh. Ohhhhhhh!" (A, 57), and says she is sure Miss Natasha is going to give her the book. Not so: "I'm no fairy godmother," the counselor briskly remarks. "Make your own pictures" (A, 57). She then takes the book and leaves.

Clara does not see Miss Natasha again. Looking for her on

the last day of camp, she asks the camp director where she is, to hear that the camp has no night counselor, and no Miss Natasha either. The director adds that years ago the camp was an Arts and Crafts camp; at that time they had a Miss Natasha who taught jewelry making but has long since died. The story closes with a paragraph of reflection from Clara: she knows she will not return to Camp Fat, because she knows that, thanks to Miss Natasha, she won't need to return.

The point of Miss Natasha's visit becomes clear to Clara after she peels all the plastic off the book and finds the lovely Clara inside. As she tells Miss Natasha, "You put all that mess on [the book] so that I would have to realize that . . . I'm fat and a little nasty and have to take all that off by myself so that people can see the beauty inside" (*A*, 57). Throughout, the tale emphasizes that the inside is where the beauty lies—and that finding the beauty can be surprising or even hard to do. Clearly evident is Konigsburg's theme of children finding their own identities, of looking at themselves "on the inside, where it counts."

Characterization—here of Clara and Miss Natasha—is as chief a focus in "Camp Fat" as it was in "Leonids" and in "Jason." Clara is again something of a smart aleck, like Lewis in "Leonids." She is better at it than Lewis, however. From first to last, Konigsburg's wit and humor appear in this tale largely through Clara's thoughts and words. See, for example, her response when her mother assures her,

> "Clara, inside every fat little girl, there is a skinny little girl screaming to get out."
> And I said, "Inside this fat little girl, there is a skinny little girl screaming, 'I'm hungry!'" (*A*, 30–31)

Clara is flip but endearing. She is not the stereotypical obese person making fat jokes, though she seems so at first. Interested in the jewelry demonstrated by Miss Natasha, she is capable of sticking to the task of peeling off layers of smelly plastic to see the beauty inside; she is ultimately capable of realizing that her own outside is "fat and a little nasty" (*A*, 57) but that she can (and will) change that.

Miss Natasha hasn't Clara's depth of characterization, but she too has her own form of wit. Once we learn that Miss Natasha died some years back, and that the story's Miss Natasha must therefore be a "ghost"—or another form of re-turnee—some of her earlier statements appear in a new light. For example, Clara has noticed her twisted fingers and asked, "You got arthritis or something?" (*A*, 40). Told "Yes" by Miss Natasha, Clara suggests aspirin. Miss Natasha replies, "I'm afraid that I'm beyond taking aspirin" (*A*, 41).

Like Clara, she is more than a wit. She leads Clara to the realization that what's inside is important, and to the realiza-tion that an unprepossessing outside can put people off. She is hardheaded too. When Clara says, "I know now, dear Miss Natasha, that you are going to give me the tiny gold book, the greatest treasure of them all," Miss Natasha replies, "No, I am not" (*A*, 57).

The interaction of illustrations and text is again important in this story. Gary Parker presents the tiny ring-watch, the opened locket, and the postage-stamp-sized book with Clara's poem and (thin) portrait. The story could omit the first two illus-trations without losing meaning, as they are described in the text. The poem, however, appears only in the pages of the "book"; no words mention the thinness of the portrait-Clara. Without the illustrations on pages 52–56 the story would have a hole in the middle.

"Camp Fat" is Konigsburg's first venture into fantasy. She has chosen to keep the fantasy secret until the close; Miss Natasha's ghostly status does not appear until the last page. The story does not feel like fantasy until that point, though Miss Natasha does seem more than normally competent as counselor and guide. As will also be the case later, in *Up from Jericho Tel*, Konigsburg's "ghost" is an interesting and intelligent adult character who also has supernatural powers that help children to pursue their identities.

The issue of "fat" is resolved more easily in "Camp Fat" than in the first comparable work to come to mind: M. E. Kerr's *Dinky Hocker Shoots Smack* (1972). Dinky (Susan) Hocker eats incessantly; she must proclaim herself a heroin addict to gain her parents' attention to her food addiction (and to the problems that cause it). There is no wise (and ghostly) deus ex machina here; Dinky's friends try to help her, and her parents eventually seem to be ready to help her, but the book closes with no guarantees. "Camp Fat" is more upbeat.

"Momma at the Pearly Gates" *(illustrated by Gail E. Haley)*

The plot of "Momma at the Pearly Gates" is simple. The fifth-grade narrator (not identified as to gender) tells a story of her/his mother, or "Momma" as she/he always writes. Momma was bused to school in her Ohio town during her fifth-grade year—bused because one of her teachers "thought that it would be a shame for all of Momma's smarts to go down to that other school with all the poor colored kids" (*A*, 62) just because her parents had moved to that part of town. Momma was also poor, and black, but her teacher got permission for her to stay in the school for the remainder of the school year. Momma took a city bus ("four cents a ride") back and forth each day between home and school. Thus she had to carry her lunch each day; she couldn't travel home at lunchtime.[3]

Momma has been going to school by bus for two weeks as her story opens. She has spent the two weeks "all alone in the Franklin School during lunch hour and enjoying it" (*A*, 65). She has also been practicing her cursive writing on the classroom blackboards during those lunch hours. After the two weeks Momma is joined by Roseann Dolores Sansevino, a fourth-grader.

The first interaction of the two little girls is unpromising; Roseann calls Momma a "dirty nigger," to which Momma replies, "Ding Dong Dago" (*A*, 69). This inauspicious beginning characterizes the relationship of the two children for the next week. During that week the two girls draw on the blackboards in the fifth-grade classroom. Roseann makes minor drawings on a side blackboard, then immediately erases them. Momma, however, embarks on a "project" (*A*, 75). She fills all (or most) of her classroom's back blackboard with a chalk drawing of Noah and the Ark. Noah and Mrs. Noah she colors in white.

Roseann, still negative to Momma's race and (therefore) incensed at Momma's insolence at drawing on a blackboard normally reserved for teachers, threatens to tell the teachers. And she does. The teachers' response is not what Roseann had expected; the teachers praise Momma for the quality of the drawing and thank Roseann for telling them about it. Then the teachers bring the entire fourth grade into the room to see the drawing. The children praise it, but repeatedly ask Momma, "Did you really? Did you really do it?" (A, 78). At that point Roseann says, "'She really did it. I watched her from start to finish.' She said it loud enough for everyone in the whole fourth and fifth grades to hear" (A, 79). Roseann has turned from adversary to advocate.

The story closes with the narrator's quoting Momma as saying that the time of her being bused was the beginning of two things. One of the things was Momma's career as an artist and illustrator of children's books; the other, says Momma to her child, "is told in the story" (A, 79).

This is perhaps the most artfully plotted of the book's four stories. Momma's writing on the blackboard early in the story has been handwriting practice modeled on a board-top diagram in a first-grade classroom; that practice, given Momma's artistic bent, allows Momma to write "Please do not Erase" (A, 75) in official-looking script at the top of her Noah picture in the fifth-grade classroom. Thus she can work on it for the three days such a major drawing project needs. Roseann's movement from adversary to advocate has also been prepared for; though she is hostile to Momma on racial grounds, she nonetheless finds Momma's Noah-drawing so interesting that she stops her own doodling on another blackboard and simply stands and watches Momma's drawing "from start to finish" through the three lunch hours the project takes.

Konigsburg's characterization focuses on Momma; Roseann speaks only 13 sentences (14 if we count a "Ha!" [A, 76]). Momma, on the other hand, has 29 sentences, plus several pages of comments reported secondhand by the narrator. Momma also appears in several illustrations, each of which shows her as black (unlike Jennifer in *Jennifer*). Her blackness is essential to her characterization. From the first page we know that Momma was not only a poor child, but also a black child. We soon learn that Momma eats her lunch "all alone, and proud to be it," which may hint at informal lunchtime segregation; we also read that Momma enjoyed the blackboards at her school so much that "that is the first time she ever thought black is beautiful" (*A*, 66). The issue of Momma's race comes to a point with Roseann's "dirty nigger" outburst; Momma is not to be vanquished with racial slurs. Not only does she return the compliment with "Ding Dong Dago" (*A*, 69), she later lectures Roseann on "Nigger Heaven" (*A*, 72).

Momma's characterization goes beyond black pride and sturdy independence, however. She is also a talented artist. Moreover, she appears as a mother who talks lovingly and patiently to her child, and tells her/him stories of the old days. In short, Momma appears characterized as personifying black pride, human independence, artistic genius, and intelligent maternal care. Konigsburg has accomplished a great deal in 18 pages.

She has, additionally, accomplished more than characterization. "Inviting Jason," "The Night of the Leonids," and "Camp Fat" each embody one or two major themes; "Momma at the Pearly Gates" touches solidly on three: black consciousness vs. racism, the need to know one's history, and—subtly stated—the ability of art to break down barriers between individuals.

The theme of black consciousness in the face of racism is obvious. Momma is black, eats alone, and is proud; the word *nigger* is derogatory in Roseann's mouth but is almost immediately paired up with "heaven" by Momma; and, most obviously, black Momma triumphs over white Roseann's racist attitude. Momma is reminiscent of Lena in Ouida Sebestyen's *Words by Heart* (1979): black, and put down for her blackness, Momma will no more surrender her personhood than Lena will allow her white opponent to win the Bible-verse memorization contest. In each case, the individual proves herself—*finds* herself—by rising above the racism of her environment, each through the use of a unique talent: memorization for Lena, drawing for Momma. The two works are also similar in that as they close the two black protagonists have each touched something in their adversaries that has compelled the adversary—Roseann and Mr. Haney—to react positively toward the black girl.

Though the racist theme is the most obvious, it is neither

the most important nor the first theme to appear in "Momma at the Pearly Gates." The first concerns history. Child psychologist Erik Erikson long ago suggested that youths need to know how they fit into time, into history, before they can fully mature. This story opens with the narrator's recounting her/his being fitted into history by Momma, which takes place in the interaction between illustrations and text. The narrator has asked Momma "what it was like back in those days" (A, 63). Momma responds in the text by citing no TV, radios that were major pieces of furniture, and a greater number of "white people [who] were poor then" (A, 63). It is the illustrations, however, that most clearly place Momma, and therefore the narrator, in history.

Gail Haley's early illustrations of Momma—illustrations that portray the way the narrator tries to picture Momma "in those days"—show Momma first as a sharecropper child picking cotton. The second portrait shows Momma in a poke-bonnet, barefoot in a field, with a hoe in one hand and a bunch of turnips (or parsnips) in the other. Both these portraits err, as Momma asks her child, "Does knowing that we had saddle shoes and zippers help any?" Her child affirms that "it helps" (A, 64), and the climactic portrait-illustration shows a young woman in white bobby-socks, saddle shoes, pleated skirt, and modish jacket—*the* fashion look of the fifties.

Konigsburg and Haley have sketched one typical history of blacks in America as they recounted the narrator's conception of her/his Momma. The illustrations move from sharecropping through rural life to the urban middle class, as one segment of American blacks has done. Konigsburg does not give words to this theme, but it is clear that the story outlines "roots" for the American black child who is likely to read this story.[4]

One would think these themes of triumphant black consciousness and racial-historical consciousness sufficient weight for any short story to bear. Konigsburg includes one more, however: the ability of art to break down barriers between individuals. It appears in the interaction between Momma and Roseann. Roseann is at first antagonistic to Momma. After Momma's drawing project, though, Roseann becomes Momma's supporter. As the illustration shows, Momma's drawing is indeed very good. It wins Roseann over despite her racist attitudes. This strength of art over racist attitudes is presumably "the other thing" that began at this time in Momma's life.

I should add that the black-consciousness theme resurfaces in Momma's discussion of the drawing. When Roseann challenges Momma's saying Noah was black with "Ha! . . . Then why did you color them in white?," Momma responds, "Because that is the way you show a black Noah on a blackboard. Black and white is how you look at things" (*A*, 76). "Black and white is how you look at things" carries a great deal of thematic weight by this time in the story; the blackboards that have been central to the narrative become metaphors.

Throwing Shadows

In the keynote speech at the Seventh Annual Conference of the Children's Literature Association in 1980, Konigsburg used Shakespeare's Caliban and Ariel from *The Tempest* to describe her intent in *Throwing Shadows* (1979). The "middle-aged child," she suggested, contains unintegrated inside him- or herself both the monstrous Caliban and the sprightly Ariel. In *Throwing Shadows* she dealt with "Five heroes, each of them a young man—somewhere between the ages of four and sixteen. Each of them in the process of recognizing Caliban and integrating him with the magic that is Ariel."[5]

"On Shark's Tooth Beach by Ned"

Ned identifies the setting of his story as "Hixon's Landing," his father's "fishing camp down on the intracoastal waterway just across Highway AIA . . . in north Florida."[6] Ned is Asian American; his age is never stated. Another character refers to him as "boy" or "son" and later implies that Ned is considerably younger than college men, so he is presumably somewhere from 8 to 14.

Ned does his share of the chores at Hixon's Landing; doing chores one day, he meets a "senior citizen" who identifies himself as "President Bob" (because he was, he says, president of a college in Michigan). President Bob has found a fossilized shark tooth. Ned tells President Bob that he has found many on the beach; he and his mother mount and sell shark teeth, in fact.

They do not, however, sell the teeth large enough to be
"trophies" (T, 8), which are special to them. Once he learns that
Ned is something of an expert in finding shark teeth on the
nearby beach, President Bob comes daily—even on Saturday,
when Ned is trying to sleep late—to dragoon Ned into hunting
for shark teeth with him.

At first Ned has to show President Bob how to identify a
shark tooth. He even gives President Bob a big tooth he finds on
one of their first such expeditions. Then President Bob begins to
find more, and larger, fossilized teeth than Ned does. This trig-
gers competition in Ned, and he sneaks away from President
Bob to do extra hunting so he can appear to be finding more and
bigger teeth himself during their regular hunts. Following one of
his solitary expeditions Ned finds a "trophy": four teeth still em-
bedded in a portion of the shark's jaw. He is triumphant. As his
mother says, "It is the Nobel Prize of trophies" (T, 24).

When President Bob comes to ask Ned to hunt for shark
teeth again, Ned allows him to see the new "trophy." President
Bob is overcome with jealousy and greed. Ned exults at the expression on President Bob's face, but then pictures to himself
the expression on his own face. Repulsed at the idea of project-
ing a similar image of greed, or of hateful smugness, Ned
abruptly tells President Bob, "It's for you . . . It's a present from
me" (T, 26).

As usual, characterization is one of Konigsburg's strengths
in this story. From the first, Ned, the chief character, speaks in
a distinctive voice. He is Konigsburg's first laconic narrator.
President Bob especially brings out the laconic in Ned; when
President Bob calls Ned "boy" or "son," Ned responds, "Name's
Ned" (T, 6, 7, 26). Not only is Ned laconic, but he speaks a distinctive dialect. He says of the sandwiches his mother sells, "She
does a right good job on them, I can tell you" (T, 4); and he uses
"somewheres" in place of "somewhere," and "smarter'n" and
"prettier'n" in place of "smarter than" and "prettier than" (T, 7).
In short, Ned's voice contributes to a strong characterization.
That same strength is apparent in his insistence on his own personhood, especially in the numerous instances of insisting that
President Bob call him "Ned," not "son" or "boy." His voice is a
strong and winning one.

Ned has his shortcomings, however. He competes with President Bob, and for a time he sinks to President Bob's level of jealousy and greed in regard to the shark teeth. Their competitiveness appears early in the story. When President Bob reports that as a college man he became familiar with sea life, Ned responds, "Oh, yeah!" (*T*, 12). Later Ned refuses to look closely at some shark teeth President Bob has found, and when President Bob outperforms him in the hunting Ned gets up early the next day and skips breakfast in order to beat President Bob in the collecting game. When President Bob beats him yet again, Ned makes a special effort and digs up many shark teeth solely for the purpose of defeating President Bob. He has sunk to President Bob's level.

He is, however, able to rise from that level. Just as he early in the story gave President Bob a large shark tooth (though certainly not a trophy), he at the close of the story rejects his own smug greed and gives to President Bob the "Nobel Prize of trophies" (*T*, 24).

Though the major strengths of this story lie in characterization and—as I later suggest—theme, Konigsburg's style again merits comment. On the last day of the story Ned rises early, ignores the sunrise (though he usually watches it), and heads for an area of beach that he thinks will yield a lode of shark teeth. He digs frenetically:

> I dug.
> I dug and I dug and I dug.
> I put all my findings into a clam shell that I found, and I dug, and I dug, and I dug. I felt the sun hot on my back, and I still dug. I had my back to the ocean and my face to the ground and for all I knew there was no sky and no sea and no sand and no colors. There was nothing, nothing and nothing except black, and that black was the black of fossil teeth. (*T*, 21–22)

Konigsburg has captured, masterfully, the single-minded greed that ignores beauty as it pursues possession. The jerky rhythm of the repeated "I dug" underlines the earthbound goal Ned seeks, as does the repetition of the "no" phrases.

Konigsburg announced that this story, like the other four in *Throwing Shadows*, concerns overcoming one's Caliban and becoming a better person. That theme is clearly apparent in the story; Ned and President Bob become antagonists early on, and Ned sinks to President Bob's level of greed and jealousy. But he recovers, suppressing his Caliban.

"On Shark's Tooth Beach" compares interestingly with other works about old-young relationships. President Bob, unlike the older characters of most such works, remains wholly unlovable. His unlovableness is exceeded only by that of the constantly sniping Grandma Bradshaw in Katherine Paterson's *Jacob Have I Loved* (1980), and Grandma Bradshaw has the excuse of senility. President Bob was, we feel, just as shallow when he was young as he is now. Konigsburg's later "At the Home" deals sympathetically with the old; here she shows that "old" need not mean "worthy of respect."

"*The Catchee* by Avery"

Avery, the narrator of "The Catchee," is a 10-year-old looking back on his life from just before Christmas in his sixth-grade year. His memoirs start with his first-grade year, the year he held his brother Orville's schoolboy-patrol flag for him and directed traffic at an intersection far from school. As he does this, he is caught by a policeman and escorted away from the intersection while the policeman lectures him on the dangers of the unauthorized directing of traffic. Orville has directed traffic without authorization in this spot for years, but Avery gets caught after raising the flag only once and letting it back down again.

While waiting for Orville to join him and go home after this event, Avery "figured out . . . life. I realized that the world is made up of two kinds of people: the catchers and the catchees. I was a catchee" (*T*, 32).

The concept of "catchee" is the thread on which Konigsburg strings the plot's episodes. Avery is caught not only directing traffic but also "mailing" a wet drink cup (he was only half-way through short vowels and thought a *letter* box was a *litter* box), breaking and entering (when he entered the home of a woman who had hired him to water her plants), and "shoplifting" (he was comparing some of his mother's panties with those in a shop so he would know the kind to buy as a gift for her).

Konigsburg's summary of Avery's characterization appears when his brother Orville suggests to him at the story's close that as a result of his "catchee" nature he is basically an honest, brave boy. Because he knows he will be caught, he knows he must be honest if he is to survive at all and is "always prepared for the worst" (*T*, 44). Instead of crying when accused of shoplifting, and instead of having his mother called and ruining his Christmas surprise for her, he calmly tells the store manager to call his brother, who will "stop here on his way home and straighten everything out" (*T*, 43). This, says Orville, shows Avery's courage.

Though this is a less profound story than the others in *Throwing Shadows*, finding its interest mostly in the plot complications Avery suffers through his "catchee" nature, there is more to the story than funny plot and minimal characterization. Konigsburg's wit again enlivens the writing, and a comment on sibling relationships also appears.

Konigsburg's wit first surfaces when Avery is caught directing traffic. He says he is sharply addressed by "a voice that wore a uniform" (*T*, 32). Later, reporting having "got lice, athlete's foot and poison ivy" all at once, he says, "The only parts of me that didn't itch were my fingernails and, every now and then, the roof of my mouth" (*T*, 35). Similar witty comments appear throughout the story.

Perhaps the story's most attractive element is its theme of sibling relationships—fraternal relationships to be specific. Orville is supportive of his six-years-younger brother after the letter-litter incident, putting his arm around Avery's shoulder and walking him home. Avery's response: "There was only one spot where Orville's arm touched my shoulder that afternoon, and it was there for only three blocks and that was many years ago, but to this day I could still point to exactly where it was" (*T*, 34). This warmth appears again at the story's close. On informing Avery that his "catchee" nature will make him both honest and brave, Orville adds, "I think you're going to be a leader of men, brother" (*T*, 44).

Avery feels very good about that. "A clarinet began playing inside me" (*T*, 44), he reports. He and his brother are close—and that closeness is a major part of this story. This sort of closeness, which was present between Claudia and Jamie in *Files* and Ben and Howard in *(George),* is reminiscent of children's books of an earlier age—*Little Women,* for example. During the past few decades problems with sibling relationships have more often been the focus of children's and adolescent literature—as in Katherine Paterson's *Jacob Have I Loved,* where two sisters, Caroline and "Wheeze" (Sara Louise) Bradshaw, remain separated by Wheeze's jealousy of the favored sibling. Still, stories of pleasant sibling relationships are being written, and not only by Konigsburg. In Ouida Sebestyen's *Words by Heart* 12-year-old Lena is not only a phenomenal memorizer of Bible verses, but she also loves and cares for her three younger siblings. Sara Godfrey, in Betsy Byars's *The Summer of the Swans,* similarly loves and cares for her retarded brother, Charlie. Cynthia Voigt's Tillerman children are perhaps the chief modern example of loving sibling relationships.

"In the Village of the Weavers by Ampara"

The "Ampara" of the title is a young woman Konigsburg has said she does not consider the protagonist of the story (Interview, January 1989). Because a male protagonist narrates each of the other four stories of *Shadows,* one may wonder why the deviation here. Konigsburg answers that question in her narrator's first paragraph: "I am Ampara, and it is I who will tell to you the story of Antonio and me. Antonio speaks in two languages, the language of Quechua and that of Spanish. I also speak in two languages, Spanish and English. Spanish is the first language for both Antonio and me, but it is English that you and I have between us, and that is why I must tell the story" (*T,* 49). It is as if Ampara had read the other stories of the book and were explaining to the reader why this story differs from their pattern. The paragraph also establishes one of the story's characterizing techniques: dialect.

Examples of that dialect abound. The above paragraph begins to focus on it. The early "it is I who will tell to you the story," though correct, would be said by no native speaker of English. A native speaker would not say "the language of Quechua and the language of Spanish," either. These dialectal usages establish Ampara's characterization throughout the story.

The plot of "In the Village" is simple. As the story opens Ampara is a novice guide; she is close to achieving "finished guide" status. As a novice she visits the village of the weavers while accompanying a "finished guide," and there she meets Antonio. Antonio, 12, is selling the large weavings normally sold only by adult males. Ampara asks why he does so, and Antonio explains that his grandfather has hurt his foot and cannot run to the plaza when the tour bus arrives.

Ampara views the grandfather's injury, thinks it serious, and fetches medicine to treat it. The medicine, and increased cleanliness, heal the grandfather, who reappears in the plaza on the day Ampara becomes a "finished guide." He is grateful; Antonio is not so grateful. Though glad his grandfather can again run to the plaza, he does not like it that he himself must now "make business" by selling shawls and pocketbooks with the women and children instead of the large weavings he had been selling alongside the adult males.

He soon remedies this demeaning situation, however. He boards Ampara's bus and travels to another hacienda. There, he is soon "making business" (selling large weavings) with tourists who come to that hacienda for lunch. Ampara allows him to use her bus in part because when he travels on it, he sings Quechua songs for her tourist groups. The tourists love the songs; the singing soon becomes an essential feature of her tours.

Especially taken with one of the songs, Ampara asks Antonio to teach her the Quechua words. He refuses, saying, "If I teach you that song, you will then sing it, and you will no longer ask me to ride the bus" (*T*, 66). Ampara, angry, thinks of refusing further bus rides to Antonio. She decides to continue to transport him, though. Her reason is not just that his singing is popular—she could have used village girls to replace him—but that she fears "that if I dismissed him from the bus, it would only make him more of the way he was" (*T*, 66). Ampara wants to show Antonio the value of graciousness.

She gets her chance when Antonio has been riding the bus, singing, and "making business" for a year. Now 13, he finds his voice cracking as he sings one day. He can no longer sing, but Ampara picks up the song where his voice has left him, and finishes it. He is amazed; that she had learned the song but had not forbidden him the bus is inconceivable to him. The story closes with his assuring Ampara that his "adult voice" will not be the selfish voice of his childhood, but a strong and gracious one instead.

As the above plot summary shows, Konigsburg characterizes Ampara and Antonio as wholly different from one another. By the story's end, it is clear that Ampara's way is the better way; Antonio says he will be a better man than he was a child, and Ampara confides her pride "that I was the guide who got him there" (T, 70). "Guide" is metaphor here; Ampara, older than Antonio, has shown him how to vanquish his Caliban and become gracious. She is almost a parental figure to Antonio, whose orphan status the story establishes in a few lines.

Antonio, in opposition to Ampara, is neither gracious nor kind. When he first speaks to Ampara she realizes, "The reason he answered me at all was because he knew that it was important to be nice to tour guides so that they will bring the buses to his hacienda instead of to another one" (T, 53). His motive for being civil, in short, is a profit motive. Moreover, on the day of two good events—his grandfather's foot is healed and Ampara becomes a "finished guide"—Antonio congratulates neither. He can only sulk because he has been relegated to "making business" in the company of the children once more.

Antonio's materialistic focus is clear. Given that focus, his refusal to teach Ampara the Quechua song is understandable; he thinks others are equally materialistic, and that Ampara only allows him bus privileges because he is economically valuable to her. When Ampara shows she knows the song but nonetheless has allowed Antonio to ride her bus and will still allow him to ride it, he is first dumbfounded, then converted: "I thought that . . . if I taught you the Quechua songs . . . you would never again ask me to ride the bus" (T, 70), he says. "I would never think in that way, Antonio" (T, 70), replies Ampara. Antonio realizes that she would not "think in that way," and that he too can think in other ways—firm but gracious ways. He resolves to become more gracious a man than he was a boy. Antonio's conversion may occur too swiftly for some readers; the swiftness of the change will for them be a weakness in Antonio's characterization.

Though the story's focus is again the male protagonist's change for the better, readers will also find pleasure in Konigsburg's technique. The description of the grandfather's injured foot is a good example of Konigsburg's strength in this area. She does not spare graphic descriptive detail: "It was cut very badly and was very ugly with pus. It was oozing all around the cut and the skin was stretched so thin from the swelling that I could see dark colors under the skin churning in the manner of the insides of an earthworm freshly turned up out of the ground. The foot itself was shapeless from swelling, and it was something ugly, really ugly to see" (*T*, 55). This is some of the strongest descriptive writing Konigsburg has done.

Overall, the story is strong, even though Antonio's conversion happens so quickly—about five minutes—that it lacks credibility. The story's theme, however, and Ampara's dialect, make it memorable.

"*At the Home* by Phillip"

Konigsburg presents a tale within a tale in this story. The framing tale concerns Phillip, the narrator. Phillip has broken his left arm ("and I am right-handed, so I had to go to school anyway" [*T*, 74]). By chance accompanying his mother to the local "old folks' home" where she is a volunteer aide, Phillip meets one of the residents, Miss Ilona Szabo, and begins to record her story of "how being so ugly saved my life" (*T*, 84). The bulk of the short story then becomes a tale within a tale—Miss Ilona's recounting of her story interspersed with Phillip's meeting other residents of the home. By the time Miss Ilona has finished her story, virtually everyone in the home has requested to have his or her story also recorded. By this point, however, Phillip's arm has healed, the cast has been removed, and he is ready to return to his normal round of activities.

How is he to satisfy the seniors' desire to have their stories preserved, while still pursuing his own life? After mulling over this problem during the last few episodes of Miss Ilona's story, Phillip finds an answer; he will put her in charge of seeing to it that everyone's story gets recorded. (The text implies, but does not state, that Phillip quietly donates his cassette tape recorder to further the recording effort.)

Miss Ilona at first resists but pretty clearly likes the idea and only wants to be argued into it. As the story closes she has agreed to undertake the project. The seniors' stories will be saved.

So much for the framing tale. Miss Ilona tells the central story in episodes. Though Phillip doesn't quite realize it, she strings out her narration in order to bring Phillip back to her side. Their relationship—a major focus in the story—grows during their talks, which often do not get around to her life story until after "she would ask me about my day and what I had learned at school, and some other days we had agreed to watch the same television programs, and we would have to discuss them when I came" (*T*, 96–97).

Miss Ilona begins her story by telling Phillip, "Come back tomorrow, and I'll tell you how being so ugly saved my life" (*T*, 84). This establishes both the episodic nature of the narrative—Phillip is always coming back tomorrow—and its guiding theme: how Miss Ilona's ugliness saved her life. Her present appearance, a descriptive strong point in the short story, makes her former ugliness believable: "The woman looked like a troll or one of those dolls that they make by drying an apple and letting it get all wrinkly. She had short frizzy hair on the top of her head, but it was so thin that each hair seemed to stand up like a tiny flag making claim to a quarter-inch of territory" (*T*, 82).

Her ugliness saved her life both during World War II and during the postwar Russian occupation of Hungary. As a Jew, she would have died during World War II, but her ugliness landed her a job as governess to a family where the wife was jealous of just about every young woman who came in contact with her husband—every woman, that is, except the young but ugly Ilona. Ilona was able to "blackmail" the wife into claiming Ilona was her (non-Jewish) cousin. Thus Ilona's ugliness saved her life the first time.

Her ugliness must have been spectacular, for it enabled her to pose as a male cook in postwar Budapest. As a male cook she was chef for "Comrade Zloty," the head of the Communist party in Budapest. That job saved her life, she tells Phillip, in two ways: it allowed her to eat and even to smuggle food to her surviving family members, and it gave her the opportunity literally to spit into "Comrade Zloty's" soup. She taught the entire Hungarian staff to join her in this ceremony, which they duly observed prior to serving Comrade Zloty's soup course:

> "How did that save your life?" [asked Phillip.]
> "It saved my soul," she said. "And that is ... part of ... how being ugly saved my life." (*T*, 106)

Soon after this exchange Miss Ilona's "story" ends. With Phillip's assistance, however, it begins again as she agrees to take charge of a recording project for the entire home.

That double plot, with its jumping back and forth from Phillip-as-narrator to Miss Ilona-as-narrator, is Konigsburg's most ambitious technical effort in *Throwing Shadows*. Phillip's presence holds both plots together (Miss Ilona tells her story to him, and he reports it to the reader), but it is her voice we hear in the sections that tell of her life. Konigsburg has not attempted to capture Miss Ilona's Hungarian accent, because (to quote Phillip), "Her accent was very complicated, impossible to imitate, even for a professional, I'm sure" (*T*, 89).

Even without the accent, Miss Ilona immediately shows a voice distinctly her own. Phillip has just met her when she says, "I hope, Phillip, that you did something more interesting to break your arm than I did. I fell in the ... bathtub, ... [a] common enough accident. I would rather have broken my arm skiing with Robert Redford" (*T*, 82–83). The same dryly witty voice appears throughout. A major part of her voice, too, is her repetition of her favorite phrase, "and so on and so forth."

Phillip, like Miss Ilona, has a voice. Part of his voice appears when he says "I'll let it go at that" (*T*, 73–74) three times in the first two paragraphs. In common with many of Konigsburg's protagonists, his voice also has elements of the smart aleck. His smart mouth gets him into trouble at times. When he meets a Mrs. Silverman, he has just left a session in which Miss Ilona said that the people in the home always complained that their children never visited them. He sees "a small number tattooed in blue on her forearm" as he meets her, but nonetheless says, "Do you have children you want to complain about?" He then learns from another resident that Mrs. Silverman's children died at Auschwitz—and he feels rotten. He apologizes immediately, which says something for his courage and goodwill.

Phillip is also characterized as growing—growing into a person who no longer sees older persons merely as beige and gray "old folks" but sees and relates to them as individuals. He sees, in fact, that "they all had a story to tell" (*T*, 102), and he arranges for their stories to be preserved.

Just as her Miss Ilona/Phillip narrative technique is more complex here than in the collection's other stories, Konigsburg has made "In the Home" more thematically rich than the other stories. A major theme of the story is embodied in Phillip's growing awareness that Miss Ilona (and Mrs. Silverman, and all the other residents of the home) are individuals. They are not living "out of time" (*T*, 83)—his first thought about Miss Ilona—but are, in fact, just as vital as the young. This point on older humans would in itself be theme enough for the story. Konigsburg adds more, however. The story also communicates a sense of history and a profound comment to the effect that everyone has his or her own story.

In presenting Miss Ilona's story of evading death in World War II (though her brother was murdered), Konigsburg has added important historical fact to her story. She adds it to the story's periphery, to be sure, but we remember that Miss Ilona's life was threatened, and her brother murdered, because they were Jews. We especially remember this in the light of the account of Mrs. Silverman's children. Konigsburg adds to her store of (peripheral) historical fact the events leading to the 1956 revolution and massacre in Hungary. Imre Nagy, Russian tactics of suppression, and the final tank-led crushing of the 1956 insurrection appear lightly sketched into the fabric of Miss Ilona's personal history. Today, when so many know no history earlier than their own dates of birth, this richness of historical presence is a welcome addition to any story.

The final theme of the story, and perhaps its major theme, is that "everyone has some story to tell" (*T*, 103). Phillip first gets the idea of recording Miss Ilona's story from almost accidentally recording the singing of Mr. Malin, a Ukrainian resident of the home. Once Mr. Malin learns that Miss Ilona is telling her life story into the recorder, he demands to be next. All the residents of the home follow suit: they all want to tell their stories. Phillip is pushed into realizing they all do have a story to tell—perhaps a story with some "boring parts," but an important story nonetheless. As "At the Home" closes, it is clear that their stories will be told: Miss Ilona and Mr. Malin have begun to record Mrs. Silverman's story, Phillip's mother says the volunteers in the home are planning to duplicate the tapes and keep copies in the home's library, and Miss Ilona comments,

> "So you might say that my being ugly saved all of our lives."
> "On tape," Mr. Malin corrected.
> "Not only on tape," Miss Ilona said, "not only on tape." (*T*, 118)

This story joins a largish group of children's works concerning young-old relationships, many of which are harmonious ones between grandchild and grandparent or, as in Charlotte Zolotow's *I Know a Lady* (1986), between young person and older neighbor/acquaintance. "At the Home," though, opens in disharmony; the youthful protagonist does not at first accept the elderly as persons. He learns better.

Many contemporary children's books that depict young-old relationships are similar to "At the Home," showing the older person(s) being rejected at first, then accepted and cherished. Norma Fox Mazer's 1988 Newbery Honor book, *After the Rain* (1987), for example, shows a granddaughter's resistance to her difficult grandfather, then her growing realization that he needs her and that she needs him. The five short stories of Janni Howker's *Badger on the Barge* (1984) all explore the old-young relationship outside the family; like Phillip, the youthful protagonists open their stories alienated in one way or another from the older person. As the story proceeds, they come to accept, often even to like, him or her.

"*With Bert and Ray* by William"

The plot of "With Bert and Ray *by William*" centers on a fantasy shared by many in our society: finding a treasure in a garage sale. William and his mother ("Ma" throughout) begin managing garage sales, or house sales, soon after the death of "Pa" (a drunkard of whom William and Ma seem well rid). They enter this field at the behest of Bert and Ray, two antique dealers whom they meet at their first sale. Ma comes to know more about antiques than these two, and, when she comes across a Chinese silk screen that the two refuse to buy or even look at carefully, she buys it.

Though all other antique dealers whom William and Ma visit likewise refuse to have anything to do with the screen, William believes in Ma's "delicate feelings" about the screen. So he takes Polaroid pictures of the screen and shows them to a curator in the Chinese collection in the Smithsonian Institution in Washington, D.C. The curator identifies the screen as rare and valuable; eventually, she induces the Smithsonian to pay Ma (and William) $20,000 for the piece.

Bert and Ray, even though they helped Ma obtain the $20,000 price by pretending to want to pay $20,000 for the screen themselves, are not happy with Ma's success. She diagnoses their unease and tells them, "It seems like I got took pretty good. . . . I found out that that there screen I sold the Museum for twenty thousand dollars was really worth twenty-five thousand. Guess I just still got a lot to learn" (*T*, 150). Bert and Ray can now accept Ma on the old terms—as their inferior in knowledge of antiques. She actually knows considerably more than they, but she prefers their friendship to their recognition of her superiority—thus her fabrication of the "twenty-five thousand" story.

The plot concludes with comments by William, who has sparked his mother's growth throughout the story. He has got her into the antique business and has persuaded her to go to the Smithsonian; now, he muses, he must "help her to find out how being grateful to Bert and Ray is something she should always be, but outgrown them is something she already is" (*T*, 151).

As the preceding paragraph begins to show, William and his mother speak in dialect (as is true for many characters in *Throwing Shadows*). The dialect is southern, and illiterate: William says of his dead father's insurance money, "The little bit he did have, didn't hardly pay for his funeral" (*T*, 121), and he reports that people attempted to get into their first garage sale before 8 A.M., "the time we said we was starting" (*T*, 122).

William's Ma is equally unlettered. As Ma arrives at the

Smithsonian, for example, she says to the curator of the Chinese collection, "We brung the screen," and asks, "Should we of carried it in?" She adds, "William and me'll just carry it on over" (*T*, 144). Their dialect is not merely illiterate, however; it is also expressive. William, the narrator, demonstrates this expressiveness several times, as when he observes of antiques, "Sometimes ugly sells real good. It depends on the style of ugly" (*T*, 131). Ma, too, can be expressive: she says of her growing skill as an appraiser of antiques, for example, "I do think that had I been city born, I might could get a job in one of these here museums. . . . I got some real delicate feelings about some of these here things" (*T*, 145).

The growth of Ma's "delicate feelings" provides the thematic center of this story. From first to last, William focuses on his mother's growing ability to recognize and evaluate antiques. Initially a manager of garage sales, then of "estate sales," Ma learns "pricing" from Bert and Ray and quickly picks up what they can teach her. She then buys books on antiques, and by mid-story she can recognize a French *panetiére* that Bert and Ray have ignorantly taken for a simple kitchen cupboard.

Ma begins in the story as "just a timid soul who says 'scuse me' to the chiffonier when she bumps into it" (*T*, 123). By the end of the story she has grown considerably. She becomes capable of doubling her asking price for the Chinese screen from $10,000 to $20,000. Perhaps more important—though William does not see its importance—she understands why Bert and Ray feel uncomfortable about her success, and is able to downplay it to give them renewed comfort with her.

The story has a dark element: the dead "Pa," who was evidently demanding as well as a drunkard, recurs often in William's narration, always in terms of "good riddance." Aside from that, however, the story focuses on an engaging relationship between son and mother. William provides his mother with the necessary impetus to begin her career in antiques, and thus stimulates her growth early in the story. If he cannot see how much growth she shows in her relationship with Bert and Ray at the story's close, he is, after all, only 12 years old. He himself still has time to grow.

Stories of son-mother relationships are too rare in children's

E. L. KONIGSBURG

fiction. Most "mother books" explore daughter-mother relationships, which is fine, but the closeness that can ideally exist
between son and mother, as is the case in "With Bert and Ray,"
is a theme in need of exploration.

Conclusion

That *Altogether* and *Shadows* are short-story collections makes
them something of an oddity in the realm of literature for
middle-aged children; short stories more commonly go to maga-
zines like *Cricket*. Good book-length collections do exist, though:
in addition to those already cited see Philippa Pearce's *The
Shadow Cage and Other Tales of the Supernatural* (1977) or her
What the Neighbors Did and Other Stories (1973). *Shadow Cage*
is a collection of fantastic stories, most having to do with ghosts
of one sort or another (one being the ghost of an oak tree, in
"Guess"). *What the Neighbors Did*, on the other hand, consists of
several thought-provoking stories about choices: Should I help
cover up a robbery by a helpless old man? Should I help cut
down a majestic tree? Should I free an imprisoned freshwater
mussel? The choices are not as easy as the questions make them
appear. In the process of choosing, the protagonists explore their
identities in a way comparable with the protagonists' explo-
rations in *Throwing Shadows*.

The five stories of Konigsburg's *Throwing Shadows* are
united by one theme: a boy's rejecting Caliban and growing toward Ariel. As my discussions of the tales have suggested, the
single theme does not hobble the stories: they remain complex. A
similar collection appeared in 1973—Kristin Hunter's *Guests in
the Promised Land*. It too has only one theme: the realization by
young blacks both that their world is dangerous to them because
of their color and that they can deal with that world positively.
The stories are well worth reading; not all of them present black
victories, but all present protagonists with that strong sense of
self that Konigsburg herself finds so important.

5

The Historical Novels

Konigsburg is interested in fiction, in female high achievers, and in art. Given those interests, one is not surprised to find she has written historical fiction about both Eleanor of Aquitaine and Leonardo da Vinci. Her achievements and his art seem logical choices for Konigsburg's attention.

A Proud Taste for Scarlet and Miniver

Proud Taste (1973), a biography of Eleanor of Aquitaine (ca. 1122–1204), appeared two years after *Throwing Shadows*. Perhaps Konigsburg had gotten into the habit of short stories in *Shadows*; she divided *Proud Taste* into four sections, or short stories, each narrated by a different speaker. The technique reminds one of the five stories in *Shadows*, each with its own narrator.

The Plot

In *Proud Taste* Konigsburg tells a story within a story. The framing story takes place in Heaven; the date is "late in the twentieth century."[1] The story opens with Eleanor of Aquitaine waiting impatiently for her husband, Henry II, to ascend to Heaven from Hell (where he has been expiating various sins). Henry's mother, the Empress Matilda of Germany (daughter of

King Henry I of England, granddaughter of William the Con-
queror, and always called "Matilda-Empress" in *Proud Taste*);
William, Henry's marshal; and Abbot Suger of France also await
Henry's arrival. Eleanor proposes that Abbot Suger tell Matilda-
Empress about the Eleanor whom Suger remembers from before
Matilda met her. Then, as all four settle down, Eleanor says,
"Come, Abbot, Mother Matilda, William, come. Let us remember
together" (*PT*, 11). This introduces three of the four narratives,
which follow in the order Eleanor has just announced (her own
is the fourth).

Speaking first, Abbot Suger tells of the marriage of Louis
VII of France to the young Eleanor of Aquitaine. The marriage
was a mixture of oil and water; the two eventually separated.
Suger tells of a monklike King Louis and of a flamboyant
Eleanor—an Eleanor with a taste "for scarlet and miniver" (*PT*,
43). Though Eleanor worked a temporary transformation of the
young Louis, he reverted to his monastic ways, and she found
him, and the French court, dull. Suger's narrative closes with
his account of Eleanor's coming to him in the Cathedral of Saint
Denis and asking his counsel.

As is the case after each of the four main narratives, the
story returns to Heaven. Suger notes he loved his earthly visits
with Eleanor, then asks what happened after he died, and why
she divorced Louis VII. Matilda-Empress volunteers both answers in one statement: "Eleanor met my son Henry, and she
fell madly in love with him" (*PT*, 73). Eleanor demurs, saying it
wasn't as simple as that, and Matilda-Empress moves between
Suger and Eleanor to begin her narrative.

"Matilda-Empress's Tale" tells of Eleanor's meeting Henry
II, of Eleanor's divorcing Louis to marry Henry (1152), and of
the first 15 years of Eleanor's life with Henry—the years prior
to Henry's affair with Rosamond Clifford. They are fulfilling
years for Eleanor. She governs Normandy, Anjou, and the
Aquitaine in Henry's absence; she patronizes poets, musicians,
and other artists; she becomes queen of England as Henry becomes king (A.D. 1154); she bears eight children; and she turns
her enormous store of energy to helping Henry rule England
while transforming its government and law courts into the seeds
of their modern counterparts. She also meets and interacts with

"Thomas Becket" (Thomas à Becket), whom she does not much like. Matilda-Empress also tells of Henry's break with Becket, and of a cheerless Easter with Henry, Eleanor, and their children. She notes Eleanor's depression, adding that she had never known Eleanor to complain before. She closes her narrative, saying she does not know what was troubling Eleanor. (We learn in the following narrative that Eleanor was depressed because Henry had turned his affections to Rosamond Clifford.) "Back in Heaven" Eleanor tells Matilda-Empress of Becket's death, then asks William the marshal to speak.

William's narrative chronicles Eleanor's split with Henry over Rosamond Clifford, her move to the Aquitaine, her encouraging her sons to rebel against Henry, and Henry's subsequent imprisonment of Eleanor (really a matter of house arrest). One of the sons' rebellions succeeded; Richard the Lion Hearted conquered Henry. Henry died, Richard became king of England, and Eleanor went free. Eleanor immediately began to endear Richard to the English, setting out on a "good-will tour" and righting "some incidental wrongs" (*PT*, 175), all in Richard's name. A "Back in Heaven" period follows William's narrative. Eleanor controls the conversation and narrates "the last fifteen years" (*PT*, 180) of her life.

Eleanor's narrative—the final one—tells of Richard's going on Crusade, of his capture in Austria, of his death in battle, and of his brother John's succeeding him as king. Eleanor concludes her chapter with her efforts to make John a better king than his upbringing would suggest and with her final act of statecraft: choosing Blanche of Castile to be the wife of Louis VIII (and thus the mother of Saint Louis). Here the story returns to "Back in Heaven" as Henry II finally appears to end the book.

The Characters

Eleanor of Aquitaine ties the four narratives together. The book opens with "During her lifetime Eleanor of Aquitaine had not been a patient woman." The reader observes her impatience as she awaits Henry II's coming in the opening "Inside Heaven" segment: she paces and she drums her fingers "on a nearby cloud" (*PT*, 4). After Abbot Suger, Matilda-Empress, and William join her in waiting for Henry, Matilda asks Suger what

Eleanor was like when young. Eleanor says, "Tell her what she wants to know" (*PT*, 10). Suger first says Eleanor became "the richest orphan in Europe" upon the death of her father, William. William having arranged for Eleanor to marry Prince Louis (son of Louis VI), that arrangement is being carried out as Abbot Suger's narrative opens.

Young Louis learns he is to be married; he travels to the Aquitaine and there Eleanor first appears: "Eleanor wore a dress of scarlet, of a cloth so fine that it looked as if it had been woven by the wind. . . . The color set off her gray eyes and fine features. Yes, Eleanor was beautiful. . . . She was lively and witty and completely without pretenses or patience" (*PT*, 21–22). Eleanor's first words to her visitors are, "Which of you is Louis?" When a speechless Louis bows before her, her next utterance establishes the quick tongue that will sound throughout the book: "Louis Capet, . . . I hope that you are as convinced as I that we both could have done worse. Much worse." As Suger then puts it, "That was the first thing that Eleanor said that Louis would not have an answer for" (*PT*, 22).

The description and incident show in small most of Eleanor's characterization in *Proud Taste*. She has a quick tongue, she loves luxury, and she is quick to act. Moreover, her considerable ability and her vengefulness when crossed will soon be revealed. She will also appear as a lover and patron of the arts, particularly literature.

The quick tongue that silences Louis appears throughout the book—for instance, when Henry II directs her not to be "Holier than thou" to him on his arrival in Heaven: "But I am *holier than thou*, Henry. I have been Up for over five hundred years" (*PT*, 200). Eleanor's tongue is not only quick but ribald. Thus when her son Henry rides his horse into her hall in the Aquitaine and begins to eat while still mounted, she states, "My duties as queen occasionally demand that I sup with a horse's ass, but I have never been asked to dine with the horse itself" (*PT*, 132–33). She orders Henry—and horse—out of the room.

Eleanor is as quick in her actions as in her words. As Abbot Suger has said early in his narrative, about the two state weddings of Louis and Eleanor, "Eleanor arranged . . . everything. She was not shy about making decisions, about giving orders, about receiving homage or receiving gifts. . . . She knew what she wanted, and she had the energy to do it all. Indecisiveness wears a person out. Eleanor was never weary" (*PT*, 24).

Eleanor's decisiveness didn't always work out well. While she and Louis, on crusade, were traveling through a mountainous part of Turkey (a part filled with enemies), King Louis had ordered the first part of his baggage train to camp on a hilltop. Eleanor countermanded his order so that the camp would be made in a grassy vale farther on. Louis and his troops arrived exhausted on the hilltop only to find no Eleanor and no camp. In the resulting confusion, the Turks swept down in an ambush. Many of Louis's troops were slain. Louis was furious at Eleanor. (Though the French did then blame Eleanor for this escapade, modern historians exculpate her. Amy Kelly blames Geoffrey de Rançon for the decision.)[2]

Eleanor's decisiveness is perhaps clearest in her divorcing Louis VII and marrying Henry Plantagenet (soon to be Henry II of England). As Matilda-Empress tells it, Eleanor had no sooner seen Henry than she decided she could love such a man. She met with him and his father and the three reached an agreement. The next spring Eleanor and Louis VII divorced; two months thereafter Eleanor married Henry. Decisive.

But not merely decisive. Even before telling of her divorce and remarriage, Matilda-Empress had characterized Eleanor as "this valuable tool, this queen, this restless beauty, this Eleanor" (*PT*, 82). Soon after her marriage to Henry Eleanor showed what a valuable tool she could be: she collected taxes, administered castles, and dispensed justice in Henry's realm during his absence. She became a new person, not only decisive but constructive. As Matilda says of her, "No longer was she the ambitious, spoiled young Queen of the Franks. Now she was energetic, and her energies were well directed" (*PT*, 93). She directed those energies to aiding Henry as he ruled England and his territories in France. Later, after Henry turned his affections to Rosamond Clifford, Eleanor turned her immense abilities to getting revenge—to helping her sons rebel against Henry. The first rebellion failed, and for several years Eleanor was imprisoned by Henry.

Following Henry II's death, however, Eleanor once again

found scope for her decisiveness and ability. She rode though
England and made friends for Richard, the new king. She made
various reforms and in general, as she puts it, "served justice" in
Richard's name. She also planned his lavish coronation and
found him a wife, a Sicilian princess. All this at the age of 67-
plus; later she raised the necessary ransom to redeem Richard
from his Austrian captivity.

When Richard died shortly thereafter, she—now 77—set out
to make John as much a king as he could be. She promptly did
for John what she had done for Richard, though perhaps in
lesser compass. Finally, as her last major act, Eleanor, aged 80,
fetched her granddaughter Blanche over the mountains from
Spain and married her to the future Louis VIII; he and Blanche
produced "Saint Louis."

So far, Eleanor seems all activity and ambition. That is not
true of Konigsburg's treatment of her, however. Eleanor also
had an aesthetic taste that governed not only a love of luxury
but a love of literature. As Konigsburg suggests in our first view
of Eleanor in her fine scarlet gown, Eleanor loved luxury. Abbot
Bernard of Clairvaux did not approve; before he would agree to
pray for her to bear a child, he lectured her on, among other issues, "her appetites for gold and jewels, for music and poetry, for
color and luxury—for scarlet and miniver" (*PT*, 43).

Luxury and literature were not greatly distant from one another for Eleanor. She was a patron of poets and other literary
artists. William reports that when she returned to the Aquitaine
she patronized not only her numerous kin but also poets and
troubadours. William also tells of talking with Eleanor as she
rode near Stonehenge while under "house arrest." Eleanor was
musing about the history of Stonehenge; William told her the
legend that Merlin set the stones there. This led to Eleanor's request for a copy of Geoffrey of Monmouth's *History of the Kings
of England*, which William gave her. Eleanor then "called for her
poets and her troubadours" (*PT*, 152) and directed them to make
Geoffrey's knights, ladies, and court more noble, fair, and
courtly, which they did. (Though history records Eleanor's role
in transforming Geoffrey's work, it does not record a meeting
with William at Stonehenge. The historical Eleanor seems to
have taken an interest in the Arthur stories much earlier than

this.)

Though Eleanor dominates *Proud Taste*, Konigsburg does give the narrator of each section his or her own voice, thus their own characterizations. Henry II is also a major character, perhaps more as personage than person. Thus Matilda-Empress reports for two pages on his founding the English Common Law and devotes another two pages to the conflict between Henry and Thomas à Becket. Perhaps inevitably, humanity is hard to find in such a historical monument.

Konigsburg gives Henry his moments, though—as when he plays "on all fours" with his sons Henry and Richard. She gives special attention to his death after his defeat in a battle on behalf of his son, Count John. Philip Augustus of France has received Henry's surrender, and Henry has received in return a list of his own barons who joined with Philip to defeat Henry. William narrates the event:

> When the list of traitors arrived, the king asked me to read the names to him. I unrolled the parchment and gasped. "Sire, may God help us."
> "What is the matter, Marshal?"
> "The first name written is that of Count John."
> "My son, John Lackland? That same John whom I loved most? That same John for whom I fought this last hateful war?"
> I nodded yes.
> "Read no more, William," he said. He turned his face to the wall and whispered, "Shame, shame. Shame on a conquered king."
> He spoke no more. (*PT*, 170–71)

Style

Konigsburg shows in *Proud Taste* her usual clever wording. The chief example appears when, describing the young John, Eleanor says to Henry, "You have seen to it that he has been raised without music; you have formed him of mucus and muscle. He either cries for what he wants, or he punches for it. Snot and sinew! There is no bone there to hang a crown on" (*PT*, 167). The alliteration and assonance of "music . . . mucus and muscle" introduce the "snot and sinew" line and create a lasting impression of the hapless Count John—King John to be.

Konigsburg likewise uses the Heaven setting of her book to develop a certain wry humor. Thus she slyly puffs her own literary and artistic professions as she makes a narrative observation early in the book about Eleanor's reward for having been a patron of the arts: "musicians, artists and poets play an important role in the admissions policies of Heaven; with their pull Eleanor had moved Up" (*PT*, 4). Konigsburg continues her wry approach to her Heaven setting in an early comment on lawyers. Eleanor says that it had taken nearly eight centuries to get enough lawyers into Heaven to plead Henry's case.

Finally, we note here, as in several of her books, an earthy strain of humor. An early example occurs before Eleanor has had her first child. Married to Louis for years and still childless, Eleanor decides to ask Abbot Bernard of Clairvaux to pray that she will have a child. Her wording as she addresses Bernard is perhaps unreflective:

> "You wished to talk to me?" he asked.
> "Yes, I did," she answered.
> "About what?" he asked.
> "I want you to give me a baby," she answered. (*PT*, 41)

Abbot Suger is scandalized: "Eleanor, please," he whispers, "surely you can find a more delicate way to phrase that" (*PT*, 41–42). Eleanor, unabashed but amused, laughs.

Konigsburg has chosen to modernize the speech of her twelfth-century characters, as we see in the above dialogue, in the earlier-noted reference to a "horse's ass," in Matilda-Empress's asking, "Doesn't every corporation display pictures of its president . . . ?" (*PT*, 94), and in William's "Monopoly, a game of business" (*PT*, 135). This speech of the modern American suburb sounds unnatural on the lips of the twelfth-century European upper class; one wishes for those dialectal devices that add the flavor of another time and place to such historical fictions as Rosemary Sutcliff's *Knight's Fee* (1960) or Marguerite de Angeli's *The Door in the Wall* (1949). An adult reader will find jarring the suburban speech of *Proud Taste*.

Themes

Like her style, Konigsburg's themes work on several levels in *Proud Taste*. The book is largely biography, to be sure, but Konigsburg has embodied several themes in Eleanor and the other characters.

Eleanor embodies a form of feminism. She is capable in her own right, not merely as a reflection of whatever man she has wedded. Thus she governs, makes reforms, stimulates art and literature, and so forth. She is not simply anti-male or pro-female, however; she is pro-individual. To be sure, she does once make a solely feminist statement, speaking of where she decided to be buried: "Of course I chose Fontevrault; it was the only abbey in all of France that housed both nuns and monks, but which had a nun not a monk as its head" (*PT*, 188).

Eleanor endorses not only (female) individualism, but art. She encourages artists, musicians, and poets and directs her poets and troubadours to refine the story of King Arthur. In sum, she clothed in beauty—in scarlet and miniver—whatever material she worked with, even Arthurian history. This theme—the importance of art—appears reflected in the book's many illustrations.

Another major theme is certainly the relationship of father and son. Konigsburg shows Henry II as loving his sons but dominating them to the point that they take up arms and rebel. She shows him loving best his son John, surely the least lovable character of the book: "It was impossible for most people to like John, but King Henry loved him . . . beyond reason, but then, all love is beyond reason" (*PT*, 142).

Finally—and daringly—Konigsburg presents Eleanor as questioning the value of a Heaven as opposed to life on earth. Eleanor feels the loss of earthly life: "Even after more than five hundred years in Heaven, Eleanor . . . still missed quarreling and dressing up. . . . Eleanor missed Henry. She missed life" (*PT*, 5). This attitude appears throughout the book. Thus, later in the book when Matilda-Empress has snappily reminded Suger of the destruction of much of his beloved cathedral, he lowers his eyes in obvious sadness. Eleanor notes that those were the days "you cried in Heaven," and Suger shushes her,

"The people of Poitiers receive the charter for their town from Eleanor of Aquitaine." *A Proud Taste for Scarlet and Miniver* (New York: Atheneum, 1973), 189.

saying, "In Heaven, one is not supposed to care for worldly things" (*PT*, 125). He obviously does care—and the contrast between the passions of earth and Konigsburg's view of a passionless existence in Heaven is clear.

Illustrations

Proud Taste is the most lavishly illustrated of Konigsburg's books. From the predominantly scarlet book jacket to the double-page layout of pages 104–5 that recounts in illustrations and captions the trip of Thomas à Becket across France, Konigsburg has devoted loving care to the pictorial dimension of this book. In the center of the jacket front (Konigsburg's own work, as are all the illustrations) is a scarlet-and-miniver-clad Eleanor flanked left and right by Kings Louis VII and Henry II. The jacket back features what looks like a medieval chapter-head illumination, with "Eleanor of Aquitaine's Tale" surmounted by a king, knight, and abbot on a balcony and with a queen and a unicorn to each side of the caption (this illumination also appears in black and white as the last chapter heading).

Many of the text illustrations either resemble or reflect medieval manuscript illuminations. The text contains 19 illustrations, including the frontispiece map of France and Britain and counting the double-page spread as three separate illustrations.

Historical Accuracy

Proud Taste is highly accurate; Konigsburg's thorough research is apparent in her treatment of Eleanor's life. Where Konigsburg leaves her sources, she does so to heighten or dramatize what is nonetheless solid fact. An example is the meeting with William at Stonehenge, which results in the "Eleanorization" of the Arthurian story. I noted earlier that the meeting is fictional, but Konigsburg has merely fictionalized a fact: Eleanor was a dominant force in popularizing "The Matter of Britain," whose center was King Arthur, as historians agree.[3]

Virtually all reviews of *Proud Taste* unite to praise both the cleverness of Konigsburg's technique and her characterization of Eleanor. The lively dialogue throughout the tale-within-a-tale, and the equally lively characterization, do cause the only other recent children's biography of Eleanor to pall: Polly Schoyer

Brooks's *Queen Eleanor: Independent Spirit of the Medieval World* (1983). Brooks's book is as carefully researched as Konigsburg's, and more widely factual, but not fictionalized. There is thus no framing tale or its equivalent here, and little dialogue—most of the book's content is reported by an omniscient historical narrator. Brooks's book is useful history, no doubt, but Konigsburg's treatment of the story will interest young readers more profoundly.

The Second Mrs. Giaconda

In one of her essays Konigsburg chronicles her move from bearing "a grudge" against Leonardo da Vinci to developing ungrudging regard for him both as painter and as person. She developed this regard after reading Jacob Bronowski's essay on Leonardo in *The Horizon Book of the Renaissance* (1961), in which Bronowski echoes Konigsburg's already formed judgment that Leonardo was a great painter.[4]

He adds an element that instantly interested Konigsburg, however: he shows Leonardo as insecure. Bronowski suggests Leonardo left Florence in 1482 to go to Milan because "he was uneasy in the rarefied, super-snobbish, intellectual atmosphere that prevailed in . . . Florence. . . . Leonardo was not a bookish man; he was not a Neoplatonist believing in ideas instead of in observation" (*"Sprezzatura,"* 255–56). Thus, Bronowski suggests, Leonardo abandoned the "bookish" milieu of Florence for Milan so he could be "indisputably the Master" (*"Sprezzatura,"* 256).

Konigsburg writes that Bronowski's article let her perceive Leonardo not only as a genius but as an imperfect human—and from that she developed an interest that led her to research his life and work. The result was *The Second Mrs. Giaconda* (1975), in which, as in *A Proud Taste for Scarlet and Miniver*, Konigsburg retains a large measure of historical truth.

Her approach is straightforward: she outlines much of the latter days of the life of Leonardo da Vinci, beginning in Milan in 1482 and closing in Florence in the first decade of the 1500s, on the eve of his beginning to paint the Mona Lisa. On that painting, in fact, Konigsburg bases her entire book. She opens with a question: "Why, people ask, why did Leonardo da Vinci choose to paint the portrait of the second wife of an unimportant Florentine merchant when dukes and duchesses all over Italy and the King of France as well, were all begging for a portrait by his hand?" She immediately supplies a response: "The answer to that lies with Salai."[5]

The Plot

The book opens with the boy Salai caught stealing. He has just cut a purse, walked hastily away, and been grabbed from behind by a quick-eyed man who saw him cut the purse. The man is Leonardo da Vinci. Salai assures Leonardo the theft was an accident: "My knife accidentally rubbed a worn place in the thong" (*S*, 10) of the purse. Taken with Salai's bold manner and beautiful blond curls, Leonardo adopts Salai for his apprentice.[6]

Though wholly untalented as a painter, Salai enjoys his life as Leonardo's apprentice/servant. His life runs along pleasantly but uneventfully until Duke Ludovico Sforza, "Il Moro," Leonardo's patron in Milan, marries Beatrice d'Este. Beatrice is the plain younger sister of the lovely Isabella d'Este, whom Il Moro wished to marry but for whom he asked too late. Beatrice is the consolation prize.

Beatrice becomes close to both Leonardo and Salai. Leonardo recognizes her great good taste and visits her often. Salai does not share Beatrice's excellent taste, but the two do share a spirit of mischief; thus their relationship begins in friendliness and grows into intellectual intimacy. Beatrice is able to tell Salai that he is rude and irresponsible, and that those qualities are important to Leonardo. Leonardo stifles such qualities in himself, Beatrice tells Salai, but he needs them.

Salai is just growing to understand Beatrice's comments when she dies in childbirth. He grieves, and expects Leonardo to grieve also. Leonardo does not. Salai cannot understand his emotionless response to the death of someone dear to Salai (and, he had thought, to Leonardo). The incident dampens the relationship he and Leonardo have had for seven years.

Shortly after this event the French invade Milan; Leonardo and Salai move to Mantua. Beatrice's sister, Isabella, lives in Mantua; she begs Leonardo for a portrait of herself. Salai cannot

bear the idea that Leonardo should do a portrait of Isabella
when he never did one of Beatrice; Salai is loyal to Beatrice's
memory. Thanks to Salai, Leonardo leaves Mantua without doing the portrait. Then, once the two have settled in Florence, a
local merchant comes to Salai and asks him to arrange for
Leonardo to paint a portrait of his "newest wife, Madonna Lisa"
(S, 138). The wife is the age Beatrice would have been by this
time, and, as Salai looks at her, he sees a woman like Beatrice:
"This was a woman who knew that she was not pretty and who
had learned to live with that knowledge. This was . . . a woman
of layers" (S, 136–37). Salai is entranced, not only with
Madonna Lisa but with the idea of Leonardo's painting her portrait. This will be a perfect answer to Isabella, he thinks. Moreover, it will be "the portrait of Beatrice that [Leonardo] had
never done" (S, 137). Most of all, it will be the best portrait
Leonardo has ever done, thinks Salai, because the subject is
sufficiently unimportant that Leonardo can relax into the
painting and allow art to rule artifice.

The opening "Why?" of the book has been answered.

The Characters

Though the third-person narrator of *The Second Mrs. Giaconda*
follows Salai's point of view throughout the work, the book focuses on Leonardo. The reader's first glimpse of Leonardo is
Salai's view of him as Leonardo seizes the young thief. Salai
looks up "into the eyes, the fiercely bright eyes, of the man who
had grabbed him. The man seemed as tall as Heaven itself, and
the man had a beard that sparkled almost as much as his eyes"
(S, 8). Leonardo's companion identifies him to Salai as "the
greatest artist, the greatest mind, the greatest engineer at the
court of Milan, and that makes him the greatest in the world"
(S, 9). Not only does this effusion fit naturally into the action, it
identifies Leonardo for a young reader who may not know of
him.

Later, the narrator again describes Leonardo, this time as a
"tall, handsome man with the brightness of God in his eyes" (S,
11). Little more of his appearance comes into the book, however;
Konigsburg is more interested in what Leonardo does and is
than in how he looks. Thus she notes he sketches "facts and

ideas" as he walks about. He does this because he "could not look at things made by God without wondering how He had made them, and he could not look at things made by man without thinking of some way to make them better" (*S*, 17). He is a looker-about—an observer—and, as Konigsburg found in Bronowski's essay, not "bookish."

Visiting nearby Pavia, Leonardo meets with bookish men from the University of Pavia; Leonardo says little. In a passage reminiscent of the Bronowski article, Konigsburg has Leonardo explain his reticence: "I have not read as many books as they have. . . . I was a grown man before I learned Latin, and I had to teach myself. If I were to express an opinion to them, they could contradict it by citing Author A in Greek and Author B in Latin. It would not matter to them that my opinion was based upon observation" (*S*, 19).

As this passage implies, Leonardo feels inferior to these learned men—feels *unsure* of himself. This uncertainty recurs throughout the book. Thus, first noting that none of his students—especially Salai—was greatly gifted, and that Leonardo liked it that way, the narrator comments, "Leonardo whose father had never married his mother. . . . Leonardo who had no fortune of his own . . . never felt . . . comfortable in the presence of dukes or of university men. This Leonardo was not willing . . . to cultivate his own replacement" (*S*, 32). The narrator suggests that Salai was the perfect, even the necessary, companion for Leonardo; Salai was a "desert of talent" who could never pose Leonardo any threat but who was "a good audience" (*S*, 32).

His lack of self-assurance leads Leonardo to avoid strong emotions. As the narrator puts it, "Leonardo chose to set himself apart—above and apart. He was never comfortable when people and emotions got too close; a human situation could show him to be less than perfect" (*S*, 104). His avoidance of emotion appears upon Beatrice's death in childbirth. Salai bears the news to Leonardo, expecting him to grieve. Leonardo merely says, "I have heard," and goes on with his book. Salai cannot understand Leonardo's detachment, and berates him for it. Leonardo rejoins, "Death is the ultimate product of life," which infuriates Salai: "How can you talk about a process when I am talking about a person?" (S, 112). Salai goes on to scream at Leonardo that he cares "more for ideas than . . . for people" and calls Leonardo a machine himself—an "idea machine," a "frozen man" whose paintings are "frozen ideas" (S, 113).

"Frozen ideas" are indeed a problem for Leonardo. As Beatrice noted earlier in the book, Leonardo does freeze in certain circumstances. For example, he has agreed to cast in bronze a gigantic horse for his patron, Il Moro. (The horse's sculpted rider is to be Il Moro's father, but the book concentrates on the horse.) He fashions a clay model of the horse, which is immense but frozen. It is not art; it is craftsmanship, following all the rules but showing none of the unruly, "wild" element that makes art.

Leonardo is not, however, a consistently cold person. When he can relax into a painting, for example, Leonardo paints portraits that show the sitter's character: thus the drawing of Isabella shows her humorless self-interest, and the faces and body language of *The Last Supper*'s apostles show the characters of each as he responds to Jesus' "One of you will betray me" (S, 99; plate in Appendix).

Konigsburg's Leonardo can be warm in person too. During his first conversation with the Duchess Beatrice, for example, Leonardo hears her say she is "plain" (S, 59). His response is piercingly thoughtful: "'You are plain, my lady.' . . . He looked at the star of Bethlehem which he held in his hand. 'What an inconspicuous flower comes from this whorl of leaves. It was the whorl of leaves that I was studying. Can you make your leaf structure more interesting than that inconspicuous flower of your face?'" (S, 60). Later, after Beatrice's death and Leonardo's coldly intellectual response to it that so shocks Salai, Salai returns to his room one evening and finds 13 scudi "For Dorotea" (Salai's soon-to-marry sister). They come from Leonardo. In short, Leonardo is capable of thinking of others, and doing for them. But not often.

Salai is keenly aware of Leonardo's character; as Konigsburg characterizes Salai, he gives much less thought to his own. He is first and foremost an opportunist, living courtierlike by fitting himself into others' moods and activities. As the narrator explains, "He could be solemn; he could be gay. He could be honest; he could be dishonest. . . . He never had a particular self-image that he wanted to present" (*S*, 104).

Salai's opportunism also makes him a thief, as appears throughout the book. From cutting a purse to taking a drawing of Leonardo's and giving it to Beatrice, Salai never hesitates to steal what he wants. He is not only thievish in his opportunism; he is also clever. Taken as an apprentice by Leonardo, Salai soon shows that cleverness. As Leonardo's youngest apprentice, he is expected to do all the chores no one else wants to do: "He had about him a cheerful willingness to do them, but he was awkward. Whatever was asked of him, he attempted to do, but the others often did Salai's small jobs for themselves; it saved time in the end" (*S*, 13). The narrator presents this comment with a straight face; the reader knows that the quick-fingered thief, Salai, is being creatively awkward to escape work.

In spite of his thievish, lazy ways, Salai is valuable to Leonardo. Salai realizes this early in the book but requires some time—and Beatrice's explanation—before he recognizes the source of his value to his master. An early instance of his musing on his role in Leonardo's life appears after he has made Leonardo laugh at the "bookish" men from the University of Pavia. The narrator first comments that Salai considers only one thing important—self-preservation—then adds Salai's own reflection that he is "supplying Leonardo with something besides loyalty and shades of laughter, something that he could not define yet, but which he knew was seated somewhere in [Salai's] attitude toward things that others—men of principle, men of wealth, men of learning—considered important" (*S*, 20–21).

Salai, in fact, lacks most of the inhibitions one learns as one becomes an adult. He is a perpetual child. This appears when Leonardo talks to Salai about how people may respond to unhappy pasts, noting that many would say Salai had had an unhappy past. Salai replies, "Not me. I wouldn't say that. I just say, 'What was, was; what is, is; what will be, will be'" (*S*, 87). Salai's childlike irresponsibility takes on almost sacramental overtones here ("As it was in the beginning, is now, and ever shall be . . ."); Konigsburg is giving considerable weight to his characterization.

Beatrice clarifies Salai's importance to Leonardo later in the book: "Your master Leonardo needs something from you. He needs your rudeness and your irresponsibility" (*S*, 92). She adds immediately, "He needs a wild element. . . . All great art needs it: something that leaps and flickers" (*S*, 93). Salai fulfills his responsibility to be irresponsible in persuading Leonardo to paint the Mona Lisa. Bringing the master to do that painting is Salai performing at his best just as executing that painting is Leonardo performing at his best.

The character of Salai might give some readers pause. He is subversive, suggesting a value in thievery and childish irresponsibility. Adults may find this characterization an affront; children will find it a delight.[7]

Beatrice d'Este, the book's third chief character, became engaged to Il Moro 10 years before the action of *The Second Mrs. Giaconda*. (Il Moro waited to solemnize the marriage because of his affection for his mistress, Cecilia Gallerani.) Beatrice, whom Konigsburg presents as plain, at first appears very much in the shadows of Cecilia and of her own sister, Isabella. In fact, after the marriage festival Il Moro sends her "first to one castle and then to another" (*S*, 50) for several months while he stays in Milan with Cecilia. In the meantime Isabella has visited Leonardo and demanded first a portrait, then a sculpture. Beatrice remains in the background.

She steps into the foreground when Salai first meets her: he sees her in the courtyard, "sitting in the sun, her hair pulled through the open crown of a wide-brimmed hat. 'I'm over here,' she [said], 'trying to get the sun to make me blond and beautiful'" (*S*, 51). Shortly after this ruefully unassuming speech, Beatrice and Salai engage in mutually satisfactory (and mischievous) conversation, establishing a relationship which continues throughout the rest of Beatrice's life.

Established as playfully mischievous, Beatrice soon comes to appear a considerable personage. Thus when she compliments Leonardo, he tells her she is "very kind" (*S*, 59). Her response: "No. . . . I am not very kind. I'm just kind. What I am very is: honest. I am very honest. And I am also very neglected" (*S*, 59). She then speaks of the neglect she receives from her husband, adds that she knows of his affair with Cecilia, and confesses she is tongue-tied in his presence. Leonardo asks if she has any quality lacking in Cecilia Gallerani, and when she responds, "A sense of fun" (*S*, 61), he suggests she capitalize on that to capture her husband's attention. Beatrice takes Leonardo's advice. She does capture her husband's attention—and his affection. As Leonardo puts it, the duke falls in love with his wife.

Il Moro is not alone in discovering a regard for Beatrice; artists, poets, and craftsmen flood to her court, where "all produced their finest works, for the young Duchess of Milan had an invisible measuring rod in her head. Everyone employed by her knew that he was not in competition with other craftsmen; he was in competition with perfection" (*S*, 68). Beatrice, in short, is highly discerning. Konigsburg does not make her perfect, though; when she is later rejected by Il Moro in favor of a new mistress, she ceases to collect only the finest works of art. She takes to accumulating all grades of (expensive) art objects instead, as if trying to replace love with rich materials.

Beatrice has not lost her "measuring rod," however. When she sees *The Last Supper*, for example, she is wholly impressed: "No one who sees this will ever be free of Leonardo's vision. From this time on every painter of the *Last Supper* [sic] will be a follower" (*S*, 106). Not long after this speech, Beatrice dies in childbirth.

Style

In common with some characters in *Proud Taste*, those of *The Second Mrs. Giaconda* are based on historical figures who spoke a medieval Romance language. Konigsburg has again given her medieval characters the speech of modern American suburbs. Salai, for example, refers to the bookish men of Pavia as "those guys" and derides them because they "could get peed on by a horse, and they wouldn't know how they got wet" (*S*, 19–20). Beatrice, in turn, speaks of her surface as a "plain brown wrapping" (*S*, 59). As with *Proud Taste*, these modern terms will sound flat to the adult ear, although they may not bother child readers.

Despite the shortcomings of the dialect, Konigsburg's wit and humor nonetheless appear, along with her feeling for the power of words cleverly used. Both wit and humor inform the passage wherein Salai, seriously hung over, wakens to the sound of pounding on the studio door and a voice proclaiming,

"Prepare yourselves." Salai is persuaded he is dead (*bad* hang-over) and that this is the Last Judgment. Once Leonardo sends him to answer the door, though, he knows he is alive: "It was only a fifty-second walk from his bed to the door, but that was all the time it took for Salai to change from gratitude at not be-ing called to the Gates of Hell to annoyance at being called to the gates of the studio" (*S*, 43). This verbal lightness is typical of Konigsburg.

Konigsburg also shows her skill with powerful wording as she writes of Beatrice's death: "At eight o'clock Beatrice was suddenly taken ill. . . . Three hours later she gave birth to a dead baby boy, and an hour and a half after that—just as a new day began for all of Milan—all the world ended for Beatrice, its duchess. She was twenty-two years old" (*S*, 111–12).

Themes

Konigsburg begins *The Second Mrs. Giaconda* with three pages of one question: Why did Leonardo paint a portrait of a Floren-tine merchant's wife when more important people were begging him to paint their portraits? She suggests an approach to an answer in the second paragraph of those three pages: "The answer to that lies with Salai" (*S*, 3). The answer, as appears above, was "a wild element" (*S*, 93),[8] which Konigsburg explains as follows: "The quality that Salai helped to give to Leonardo [was] the quality that . . . Renaissance viewers demanded . . . —that works of art must have weight and knowing beneath them, that works of art must have all the techniques and all the skills; they must never be sloppy but must never show the gears. Make it nonchalant, easy, light. The men of the Renaissance called that kind of excellence *sprezzatura*" ("*Sprezzatura,*" 261). *Sprezzatura* appears in *The Second Mrs. Giaconda* as Beatrice tells Salai of his necessary role in Leonardo's life—to supply "a wild element." Beatrice develops those comments as she adds that the beginning of *The Last Supper* is auspicious: "Even in outline, [*The Last Supper*] has the beginnings of greatness in it. . . . Leonardo has allowed his mind to idle a little and let in something fresh and wild" (*S*, 93).

The "wildness" embodied in Salai eventually leads to Leonardo's painting the Mona Lisa. This appears at the book's close, when Salai meets "Mr. Giaconda" and receives his request for a portrait of his wife by Leonardo. It is there that Salai realizes Leonardo would do a fine job on the wife's portrait, because she (and her husband) were not important to him. Leonardo could let his wildness flicker as he painted the work.

Another theme is partly a reflection of Konigsburg's own interests: art is central. Plot, characterization, and theme unite to suggest art's importance, and to these elements Konigsburg adds penetrating critical comments about Leonardo's paintings. An example appears in the narrator's pointing out that the ermine Cecilia Gallerani holds in her portrait mirrors her expression. The comment opens a fruitful line of thought about predators, hunters, and so forth.

Illustrations

Konigsburg generally illustrates those of her own books that are to have pictures. In *The Second Mrs. Giaconda*, however, she chose to reproduce a bust of Beatrice and eight Renaissance paintings, seven of them by da Vinci. One—the Mona Lisa—is fittingly the frontispiece, and the others appear in an appendix. All the chief characters are represented in statue and paintings (Salai also appears on the jacket), allowing the reader to see Salai's curls, Isabella's self-absorption, or Cecilia's smugly lovely self-satisfaction.

Historical Accuracy

As in *A Proud Taste for Scarlet and Miniver*, Konigsburg has taken pains to make *The Second Mrs. Giaconda* historically accurate. In *"Sprezzatura"* she mentions having read, in addition to Jacob Bronowski's essay about da Vinci, Kenneth Clark's *Leonardo da Vinci: An Account of His Development as an Artist* (1967). Bronowski's chief contribution to *The Second Mrs. Giaconda* was his presentation of da Vinci as an imperfect human; Clark, however, provided much of the historical detail and characterization (compare, for instance, *Giaconda*'s comment about sculpture [*S*, 48] with da Vinci's note in his *Trattato* [Clark, 83]). Konigsburg has reproduced the note faithfully, though in a fictionalized context. In short, and thanks in great part to Clark's book, Konigsburg has retained historical accuracy as she fictionalized da Vinci and his peers.

As with Eleanor of Aquitaine, children's books on da Vinci comparable to *The Second Mrs. Giaconda* are nonfiction. Margaret Cooper's *The Inventions of Leonardo da Vinci* (1965) reproduces from da Vinci's journals drawings that reflect interests ranging from botany to city planning to war machines and flying machines. Cooper's book will fascinate any child with a mechanical turn of mind, who will find in its pages a side of da Vinci that Konigsburg does not emphasize. More directly comparable is Elizabeth Ripley's *Leonardo da Vinci* (1952), a straightforward biography with the barest mention of Salai as da Vinci's unnamed "favorite pupil."[9] Ripley presents da Vinci from his youth (12 years old) to his death in 1519. Although the content is interesting—as any life of da Vinci must be—Ripley's writing is transparent, using no technique or dialogue in depicting the artist. The book is richly illustrated, however, largely from da Vinci's journals and sketchbooks.

Conclusion

In both *A Proud Taste for Scarlet and Miniver* and *The Second Mrs. Giaconda* Konigsburg set herself the task of presenting a historical personage, and a great deal of historical fact, in a way that would engage her young audience. Her tale-within-a-tale technique in the one and Salai-narrator technique in the other are indeed engaging, as is the drama found in each book. Her normally sensitive ear for dialect may have suffered in these books, but the history and the personages of the history are compelling.[10]

6

Freeing the Imprisoned

Andrew J. Chronister, the protagonist of *The Dragon in the Ghetto Caper* (1974), and the brother-sister combination of Winston Carmichael and Heidi Carmichael in *Father's Arcane Daughter* (1976) are prisoners. Andrew's prison is a ghetto—an upper-middle-class suburban ghetto. Winston's is a shadow of fear and the need to care for his handicapped sister. All three children, with considerable effort and some crucial help, make their ways to freedom.

The Dragon in the Ghetto Caper

Like Maurice Sendak, Konigsburg writes of the importance of wildness: the eponymous George represents a "wild point of view"[1]—a point of view essential to Ben's creativity; Salai does the same thing for Leonardo in *The Second Mrs. Giaconda*. In *Dragon* the metaphor for wildness becomes a dragon. Konigsburg's characters pursue (or evade) this dragon through *two* ghettos. As the book ends, one realizes that Konigsburg has written about creativity and about the concurrent need for control—but not too much control. She has also written about the suburbs, as she said in her Newbery Award speech in 1968 that she intended to do. The suburbs in *Dragon*, however, are of a different sort than those in *Files, Jennifer, Bagels,* or *(George).*

111

These suburbs need a dragon.

The Plot

Dragon opens by introducing 11-year-old Andrew J. Chronister, resident of the exclusive Foxmeadow, a suburban development. Andy regularly skips his music classes and goes to his school's art room where he draws dragons (or, sometimes, constructs them from paper and burlap): "Dragons, however, were not Andy's true passion; crime was" (*D*, 3). Andy plans to become a detective, only he lacks two of the necessary elements: a crime and a sidekick. He is willing to wait patiently for the crime, but he actively seeks a sidekick. One appears, at first only an admirer of Andy's art: Edie Yakots.

In the best detective tradition, Andy addresses Edie as "Yakots." She is an unlikely sidekick—unlikely not only because she's an adult female but also because she's unconventional. Unlike the "cool" inhabitants of Andy's world, "Edie never cared if her enthusiasm showed" (*D*, 31). Moreover, she talks constantly about dragons. She embarrasses Andy, but he likes her and accepts her as his sidekick. He even sees to it that she and her husband get an invitation to the upcoming wedding of his sister, Mary Jane.

Having found a sidekick, Andy awaits a crime. While waiting, he accepts Edie's invitation to ride with her on Thursdays as she gives rides to Sister Henderson, a black woman who belongs to the church where Edie bought a used pew. Sister Henderson makes weekly collections that Andy assumes to be church collections.

It is in Sister Henderson's ghetto that Andy finally finds a crime. On one of their collection trips, Sister Henderson tells Andy that two men are waiting in a car and that they want to take "mah donations for the entire week" (*D*, 68). Andy is thrilled. His plan to catch the two—or to have them pursue him so that he can evade them—does not immediately take shape, however; instead, Edie evades the supposed robbers. The three then safely continue Sister Henderson's collection tour.

The following week the two "robbers" again appear. This time they confront Andy. He has taken Sister Henderson's collections to two black men in the house where she always delivers the money; on his way back to Edie's car, Andy is approached by the two "robbers" (white men), who want to know what he has in his pockets. As he stalls, Edie drives up and tosses sacks of rice at the two men. She and Andy escape in the resulting confusion. Edie has seen that the two have guns. Andy is sobered; guns were not in his plans.

The robbers retire into the background for Andy as events at home quicken their pace: his sister's wedding is about to take place. The intense preparations, especially for the home reception, include hiring two detectives to watch the silver, the guests' furs, and other valuables. During the reception Andy drinks his first champagne: four glasses. He staggers upstairs, vomits, and falls asleep.

He is awakened by voices in the next room. One of the voices is Edie's; as he listens fuzzily, he becomes aware that the other two voices are those of the two "robbers." Groggy but gallant, he goes to Edie's defense armed with cans of deodorant and hair spray from the bathroom. Though he temporarily sidelines the two "robbers" by spraying them in their faces, Edie refuses to run to get the detectives his father hired.

It soon becomes apparent that the "robbers" are in fact the two off-duty city police detectives hired by his parents; Andy's previous acquaintance with them was gained while they were on duty, investigating an illegal numbers game in the ghetto. Sister Henderson, they explain, is a numbers runner; she is not collecting for a church. The house where Andy delivered the "donations" is the center for the numbers racket in that area.

Andy is confounded. Not only has he finally found a crime, he has inadvertently helped commit it, and now the detectives tell him that it is his duty to help apprehend the criminals. The criminals not only include the two men in the house, but Sister Henderson, whom Andy likes and respects. Andy does not know what to do. Edie tells him: he must draw identifying portraits of the two men to whom he delivered the "donations." He does, and the two men (and, presumably, Sister Henderson) are later arrested.

The story ends with Andy deciding that he doesn't like detecting. Not only did he end up participating in the crime, but he doesn't like the arrests resulting from its being solved. Andy realizes that he needs not crime but dragons. He visits Edie to tell her he understands how she has led him away from his detective interest and into understanding what is important to him. He has not seen Edie during the days he was considering all this; he finds that her appearance has changed. She is pregnant, and planning to call her baby "Andrew" (*D*, 124).

The Characters

The chief characters of *Dragon* are, of course, the odd couple of Andy and Edie. Sister Henderson, though a lesser character, is nonetheless important to the story.

Eleven-year-old Andy's most obvious characteristic is his frequent conversational use—more than 20 times, in fact—of "for God's sake." Characteristic of Andy on a more profound level is his affinity for dragons. As we learn on the first page, Andy "does" dragons and has been doing so since third grade: "I do only dragons. They're what come out" (*D*, 54). He has been going to the art room instead of music class for about three years, thanks to the permissive attitude of school authorities.

As characteristic of Andy as his dragons, and a major plot element, is his intention to be a detective. Part of his training is to be observant, which he practices by looking around in people's houses when he collects for various charities; the other part is to be cool. "Cool" is important to Andy; it seems to involve showing as little enthusiasm as possible (e.g., Andy is embarrassed when Edie waves enthusiastically as she meets him at school). Moreover, though he is glad to hear her say she waves so violently because "she was always so glad to see Andy that her enthusiasm overcame her training," he is too cool to show he's glad to hear it. One occasion, though, shows him abandoning the cherished quality. When Edie presents him with three hand-painted eggs—Ukrainian *pysanky*—he tells himself to "stay cool": "'They're neat,' he said. He cleared his throat and added, 'They're very neat. You might even say that they're extremely neat.' . . . He looked up and caught her eye. 'Oh, well, Yakots, these are absolutely the most gorgeous Easter eggs I have ever seen in my entire life'" (*D*, 58–59). Andy's coolness suffers around Edie.

Both Andy's desire to be a detective and his insistence on

being cool vanish at book's end. He finds that he does not need "crime" to enrich his life but, rather, "difficult, strange and awkward" (*D*, 121–22) elements such as dragons.

If Andy's "for God's sake" is his verbal identifier, Edie's is what the narrator terms her "verbal confetti." It appears when Andy visits Edie to negotiate the sale of a dragon painting. During their conversation he says he likes her home, to which Edie replies, "'We thank you very much. . . . My husband is out of town. That's where I want to hang him. His name is Harry,' she said, pointing to a spot over the sofa. 'How much would it take?'" (*D*, 14). Her references here alternate between her husband and the picture of a dragon. This sort of verbal confusion typifies Edie's discourse whenever she speaks with strangers.

Edie and her husband have recently moved to Foxmeadow, where Edie fits in not at all. One of the early illustrations—of Edie and two ladies of the Foxmeadow Garden Circle—shows her uniqueness. The Garden Circle is visiting the school art show. The two Garden Circle ladies are slender, even skeletal, and are conversing but not smiling. They wear skirts (or dresses) and face away from the art exhibit as they talk together. Edie faces away from them, looking at the exhibit. She is smiling at Andy's dragon. She wears a sweater (displaying a decidedly feminine figure) and slacks or blue jeans baggy at the knees.

In addition to contrasting sharply with the Garden Circle ladies, Edie also contrasts with Andy: he strives to be cool, whereas she shows every emotion. This appears early in the story, when she waits outside Andy's school to take him with her to drive Sister Henderson on her collection rounds. Whereas most pickers-up come up the drive and wait in their cars, Edie parks her car (in the others' way), gets out, stands waiting at the door, and taps Andy on the shoulder to show she is there. She also announces herself to him, "Here am I, your sidekick" (*D*, 23). Andy is monumentally embarrassed.

Harry, Edie's husband, is an airline executive and travels all week. His absence allows Edie considerable time to spend with Andy during the course of *Dragon*. One might expect Andy, with his craving for coolness, to be repelled by Edie. He is not, for he considers his classmates "all so much alike that they could have interchangeable parts." Edie, however, "was different, bordering on strange" (*D*, 33–34), and he likes her as different. He is not above commenting on her lack of normalcy, but she deftly turns him, as when Andy has just accused her of talking "half the time . . . as if you were born without conjunctions," to which she replies, "I talk perfectly all right after people know me. Harry—he's my husband—says that I taper toward normal. I think it's nice that he says that I taper toward normal. Means that normal is less than what I usually am" (*D*, 36). As Andy recognizes, Edie *is* superior to the norm.

Part of her superiority, to Andy, is that Edie appreciates Andy's dragons as no one else has. When he gives her a dragon valentine, for example, she smiles in a way that says "Thank you" more eloquently than words. Edie likes dragons and understands that they are essential. Thus she gives a dragon pillow as a wedding gift to Mary Jane because "she should have a dragon . . . she's such a nerd without one" (*D*, 64).

Edie also understands that dragons must be controlled. She shows that understanding late in the story, when the police detectives ask Andy to describe the men running the numbers game. Edie tells them Andy can do better than a description: being "an artist," he can draw the men. Andy protests that he can only draw dragons. At Edie's urging, however, Andy finds he can draw the men. Edie leads him to control his dragon by drawing something other than a dragon.

Edie, then, is a teacher, even a nurturer, for Andy. In fact, Edie has understood what he actually needs and has helped him find the crime he seeks so he can realize he doesn't need that. She may have known about the numbers game all along, but she never quite let her left hand know what her right was doing, just so she could help Andy learn about dragons. Edie helps, nurtures Andy throughout the story. As the book closes, Konigsburg introduces another metaphor for nurture. Edie tells Andy she is pregnant. She and Harry are thinking about naming the baby Andrew—or perhaps Andrea. She adds, "Either way, it'll be Andy" (*D*, 124).

Compared to Andy and Edie, Sister Henderson is a minor but important character in *Dragon*. Her importance to the plot is evident; her identity and culture make her important to theme as well. She has her own way of talking and a distinct dignity. Her unique dialect is revealed when she points out the car in which the two men Andy thinks to be robbers await their chance to take her "donations": "See that gray Plymouth restin' down the road a piece? That ain't no ornary [*sic*] car. That car means gray evil. That man behine [*sic*] th' wheel is waitin' for me. He be waitin' for me to colleck, then the minute Ah be finished, he'll grab me, and there'll go mah donations for the entire week" (*D*, 68).

Sister Henderson is more than a dialect, however. Her quiet self-assurance in her African-American identity impresses Andy, as we can see in her response to Andy's wishing her a good "National Black History Week": "Ah don' hol' too much with Black Hist'ry Week. Ah figgers it's like white choc'lit, somethin' that started out black bein' converted inta somethin' white, an' t' me, it always taste a li'l bit waxy" (*D*, 50–51).

Style

As in all her books, Konigsburg adds to plot and characterization both wit and deft wording. An example appears in a satirical comment about upper-middle-class suburban parenting. Andy is discussing his desire to become a detective, and deploring the lack of crime in Foxmeadow:

> "I begged my father to move into a high crime area, but he refused. He says I've got to be protected because he and Mom don't have much time."
>
> "Oh, I'm so sorry," Edie said. "What is it? Cancer? Heart condition?"
>
> "No. Nothing like that. Golf, a busy law practice for my dad. With my mother, it's tennis and clubs." (*D*, 21)

Similarly wry passages appear throughout the book, usually in presentations of Foxmeadow life.

Themes

As ever for Konigsburg, the protagonist's search for identity is *Dragon*'s chief thematic concern. Ghettos of one kind or another and the importance of seeking out the unfamiliar and the unconventional—here embodied in dragons—are other themes. Edie combines ghettos and dragons to help Andy find his identity.

The book's depiction of two ghettos is not immediately apparent. At first it seems that the impeccable suburb in which Andy lives defines by contrast the ghetto nature of the area in northern "Gainesboro" where Sister Henderson dwells. Edie soon plants the idea that Foxmeadow is just a different, wealthier brand of ghetto. When Andy asks Edie if "the northern part of town" is where one finds the ghetto, she replies, "One of them" (D, 21). Later, Andy asks Edie if she thinks the (black) ghetto will be celebrating National Black History Week. She thinks not. Their dialogue is instructive: Andy opens by observing,

> "If I had a culture, . . . I'd sure celebrate."
> "You have a culture."
> "I mean a ghetto culture, for God's sake."
> "You have a ghetto culture."
> "How can you say that, Yakots? I've lived in Foxmeadow all my life. Foxmeadow has no culture. Everyone here is *unanimous*." (D, 49)

The passage implies that Foxmeadow is not only a ghetto but a culturally deprived one—a ghetto of "interchangeable parts" (D, 33), as Andy has mused earlier.

Presenting Foxmeadow as a ghetto produces a twist on Konigsburg's long-cherished setting for her works. In her 1968 Newbery Award acceptance speech she said that she wished to write of suburbia—of real suburban life. In *Dragon*, however, she writes of cloistered suburbia, of ghetto suburbia. The narrator reports early in the book that Foxmeadow is "closed"—"a ring of houses built around acres and acres . . . of a championship golf course. . . . A fence circled all around it, and a security guard was posted at the only gate. The guard checked cars to see if they belonged" (D, 41). Foxmeadow sounds more like a minimum-security prison than a suburb.

A biting example of suburban pettiness is Mrs. Chronister's suggesting that Edie's husband was "old enough to be her father," that he may have "another family tucked away somewhere," and that Edie has painted her walls in "odd colors" (D, 42–43). This "ghetto" gossip passage is a tour de force.

Dragons first appear in the book's second paragraph and last appear 51 words from the end, when Edie says that her yet-to-be-born child will know about dragons from the beginning. In the intervening 121 pages, the major characters—especially Edie—mention dragons continually. These metaphoric dragons both oppose Foxmeadow values and promote what Foxmeadow ignores or evades (e.g., the black ghetto); they particularly oppose the "coolness" Andy thinks he seeks in his life.

Andy's "doing" dragons brings about his meeting with Edie, who wants to buy a dragon painting. From that point on, Edie "does" more dragons than Andy. During their first conversation, for example, Edie says, wistfully, "Sometimes here you have to go out to find a dragon" (*D*, 21), which is why she was surprised to find Andy's dragon inside Foxmeadow, on the walls of his school. Even this early in the book "dragon" is becoming a recognizable metaphor—though for what is not yet clear. It is clear, though, that Edie sees dragons and Foxmeadow as opposites.

Andy often feels enthusiasm, though he resists it, when he associates with Edie. The chief example here has to be the already-mentioned *pysanky* episode, in which Andy abandons his cherished coolness in his delight at the hand-painted eggs. The episode goes on to imply the need to control the dragon—to control enthusiasm and creativity. That need for control appears in Edie's explanation of what *pysanky* are. She explains their Ukrainian origin, then says someone must make them at Easter or "the chained monster" will break out and destroy the world. Andy immediately identifies the chained monster as a dragon. Edie's response: "Dragons are everywhere. . . . The dragon is a necessary creature. You've got to know your dragon, but you've also got to keep him under control. That's why I make pysanky every Easter" (*D*, 60).

Soon after the above conversation Edie explains to Andy that "a nerd is a nonperson. A person without dragons" (*D*, 64). A dragon is "necessary" for personhood, then, but it must be controlled. The necessity for control appears toward the close of the book, in an earlier-noted incident. Asked to draw a picture of the men collecting the numbers money, Andy protests, "I only draw dragons." Edie persists, however, then kneels in front of him so that their eyes are level. She says, "You can do it, Andy. Know your real dragon" (*D*, 118). Andy does the drawing. The dragon metaphor includes self-knowledge, it would seem—and self-control.

The dragon is not wasted on Andy. As the book comes to its close, Andy sees that he wants dragons as much as his sister does not. Like Edie, he realizes, he needs "some monster/mystery, some mystery/monster in his life": "the important parts of life"—at least of Andy's life—are dragons. He had been seeking mystery in crime, but he has just learned—thanks to Edie—that he doesn't like crime; he likes mystery. He doesn't like "cool" either; he likes enthusiasm. Elated at his discovery, he runs to Edie's house and immediately tells her, "I know about dragons" (*D*, 123). And so he does.

The dragon metaphor states the theme of this book. Dragons are, as Edie would say, dangerous, lovely, and necessary—and they free Andy from a cool approach to life that never catches fire at any idea. They also usher him into an identity of his own.

Illustrations

Konigsburg has illustrated *Dragon* in pen and ink as she did earlier books. Several of her drawings serve solely to illustrate—that is, they simply show the action of the text and picture characters and setting (e.g., a drawing of Andy and Edie driving in her car, with a section of the black ghetto in the background, and the lively illustration of Andy spraying deodorant into the face of the detective he takes for a robber).

Other drawings both illustrate and comment subtly on themes or characterization. The cleverest shows Andy's design for the pillow Edie embroiders in needlepoint as a wedding gift for Andy's sister, Mary Jane. The drawing shows a collar-wearing dragon lying comfortably sprawled at the foot of a tree and encircled by a low fence. The initials "M" and "A" appear above the dragon, on each side of the tree trunk, presumably representing the names of Mary Jane and her bridegroom, Alton. Probably the sight of the dragon enclosed by a fence and wearing a collar would alone communicate the idea of the necessity of controlling one's dragon, but because Konigsburg has chosen to adapt the design of the last of the famous Unicorn Tapestries, the message is clear. That tapestry of the seven now hanging in

DESIGNED BY,
ANDREW J. CHR.

Needlepointed by,
Ms. E. YaKots

The unicorn enclosed becomes the dragon controlled. *The Dragon in the Ghetto Caper* (New York: Atheneum, 1974), 65.

the Cloisters Museum in New York City depicts a unicorn lying in the position Konigsburg has given the dragon. The previous six tapestries show the unicorn as wild, even violent; in the seventh it has passed beyond violence. It is at rest, calmly contained inside the fence.

Konigsburg, a former New Yorker, is clearly aware of the symbolism of the Unicorn Tapestries.[2] By using this last of the tapestries as Andy's design, she has subtly underscored her comments on dragons: like unicorns they are exotic and wild, and they must eventually be controlled—like the dragon that would destroy the world were it not for Ukrainian *pysanky*. Andy learns all this in the course of *Dragon*.[3]

Comparable Fiction

Most "ghetto" books concern minorities and the difficulties they meet in their ghettoes. The black American ghetto experience is depicted, for example, in Kristin Hunter's *Guests in the Promised Land* (1973) and Virginia Hamilton's *Sweet Whispers, Brother Rush* (1982); the Hispanic American ghetto figures in Nicholasa Mohr's *Felita* (1979). Few children's books attack head-on the values of a major group of book buyers—the white, suburban upper middle class—and consequently white ghettoes have gone largely unexamined.

An exception, however, is Louise Fitzhugh's *Harriet the Spy* (1964). The values of Harriet Welsch's parents compare favorably with those of Andrew Chronister's: the Welsch ghetto includes a brownstone on East Eighty-seventh Street in Manhattan, the private "Gregory School," and a psychiatrist to unravel the troubled psyche of daughter Harriet. The Welschs' conversations, too, mimic the "ghetto" gossip of *Dragon*.

Father's Arcane Daughter

Andrew Chronister had to leave suburban Foxmeadow to find a dragon—to find mystery, as he concludes. *Father's Arcane Daughter* involves a mystery too (one meaning for *arcane* is "mysterious," as Konigsburg's narrator points out on the last page).[4]

The reader immediately realizes that *Daughter* departs even from the broad range that earlier defined Konigsburg's norm. The jacket—Konigsburg's only illustration for the work—is the first hint. It shows five identical casement windows. In the leftmost window (on the back of the jacket) appears no one. Moving right to the second window we see someone's left arm, hand, shoulder, and fringe of hair. In the third window appears, in addition, part of a woman's face and chest (she wears a loosely draped dress reminiscent of a cassock). In the fifth window appears her entire head and torso. Her right shoulder is higher than her left, which could represent either a misshapen appearance or her leaning on her right hand as she reaches forward with her left. She appears to be leaning on the windowsill, or perhaps on a desk or table just behind the windowsill. The coming-into-view process causes her to seem to materialize out of the shadow behind her. It almost seems the five windows are five filmstrips or overlays for a cartoon camera. On the basis of the title, one assumes this female figure to represent "Father's arcane daughter," and her appearance—and bit-by-bit manner of appearing—do give the impression of mystery.

The first nine paragraphs of chapter 1 appear in italics (quoted here in full):

> *Later—much, much later—when we both knew what we had bought and what it had cost, she said that I should tell it.*
>
> *"But," I protested, "there are some parts that I hardly know and other parts that I don't know at all."*
>
> *She smiled. "Life's like that. A little knowing. A lot of not knowing."*
>
> *"My telling will be a string of incidents. Like the separate frames of a comic strip. Besides," I said, "I'm bound to give myself all the good lines."*
>
> *"A mood can be an incident," she said.*
>
> *"Oh, no!" I protested. "No, no, no, no, no. Moods are colors."*
>
> *"The comic strips are colored on Sundays. And in books."*
>
> *I thought a minute. "For me it all began on a Thursday, a September Thursday in 1952."*
>
> *"Begin it there," she urged. "That Thursday is a good place to begin. It is precise. You'll see, the rest will follow." (F, 3–4)*

We encounter two mysteries on the book's first two pages: Who are the "we" of the first paragraph? And what has been bought? In this passage we learn that the book's events are to be narrated by a character and that the narration will be "a string of incidents" (i.e., episodic). We encounter a reference to "comic strips," which may remind some of the jacket illustration, and adult readers will realize that this book, to some degree, is "metafiction"—fiction about writing fiction.

The metafiction is apparent from the (fictional) italicized conversation, which forecasts the form *Daughter* will take. The italicized conversation also establishes a major fact of the narrative—that this book will be a series of flashbacks. The narrator, living in present time, will look to the past for the incidents of the plot. We soon learn that each chapter through chapter 11—each flashback incident—begins with an italicized passage that discusses or at least refers to the incident just recounted, then points forward to the upcoming incident. The technique is reminiscent of the "Back in Heaven" sections of *A Proud Taste for Scarlet and Miniver*. The first incident will take place on "a September Thursday in 1952."

The Plot

It was on that Thursday in 1952 as Winston Carmichael and his handicapped 10-year-old younger sister, Heidi, were playing the "Invisible Game" (*F*, 6) that a woman came to the door, rang, and asked to see the absent Mr. Carmichael. Learning he is not there, she leaves, answering the butler's "Whom may I say is calling?" with "This is Caroline" (*F*, 8).

The woman returns that evening to greet Mr. Carmichael with "Hello, Father, I'm home" (*F*, 10). The next chapter outlines the events that led up to this greeting. Seventeen years ago Caroline Carmichael had vanished—kidnapped. Mr. Carmichael had never given up hope that Caroline would return. His first wife, Caroline's mother, did give up hope; Mr. Carmichael implies she drank herself to death. He then married Grace, later to be the mother of Winston and Heidi. Meanwhile, Caroline tells Mr. Carmichael, she escaped her abductors and went to Ethiopia, working as a nurse for 17 years.

Chapter 3 shows Caroline moving into the Carmichael residence, establishing her identity, and winning Winston's heart. Moreover, Caroline begins to grow close to Heidi. "Heidi"—a

nickname for Hilary given by her mother—is severely handicapped: her hearing is greatly impaired and she is physically
uncoordinated. Winston, and his family, have assumed that
"Heidi" is brain-damaged. Caroline talks with her and finds that
Heidi understands what she reads, and that she reads poetry
well beyond the level one expects of a 10-year-old. Caroline mentions this to Winston, who becomes jealous; Heidi, responding to
Caroline's approval, tries for greater normalcy in her move-
ments and actions. Soon thereafter Caroline moves out of the
Carmichael home into her own apartment.

From that base, Caroline begins to take Heidi/Hilary to a
psychologist for testing. The testing establishes Heidi's extraor-
dinary intelligence. Winston again becomes jealous of Caroline's
involvement with Heidi. Caroline explains that Heidi needs help
to establish her personhood; she, Caroline, is undertaking a
course in "special education" as part of her plan to help Heidi. It
is only by freeing Heidi/Hilary, she continues, that she can help
Winston find his own freedom. Meanwhile, Grace Carmichael
has decided that Heidi should have no more to do with Caroline,
whom Grace detests. Winston reflects on these events, and
again wonders, Is Caroline really a Carmichael?

At Grace's demand, Mr. Carmichael forbids Caroline to invite Heidi to her apartment. Caroline refers to Mr. Carmichael's
act as cowardice; Winston, angered, says, "If you were really his
child, you wouldn't call him a coward" (*F*, 94). Caroline, weary of
the identity question, promptly hands Winston an envelope that,
she tells him, holds "the evidence that establishes . . . whether I
am Caroline . . . or whether I am not" (*F*, 95). He soon tells Heidi
of the incident and shows her the envelope.

Heidi/Hilary grabs the envelope and says, "Don't open it" (*F*,
96). She asks Winston instead to disobey their father and
mother and take her to Caroline. Winston does as she asks. Caroline invites the psychologist to join them, and psychologist and
Caroline together tell Heidi/Hilary that she cannot achieve normalcy but that she can develop her mind and "overcome her
disabilities" if she is willing to "really work" (*F*, 98).

Chapter 12 opens without an italicized section. The book has
moved into the present, 23 years later than the events of the
earlier chapters. Caroline has just died. The "she" of the itali-

cized conversations is identified as Hilary, who has "really worked" and has overcome her handicaps. Hilary and Winston, seated in her office, discuss the long-sealed envelope, then open it. It contains the prekidnapping intelligence test scores for Caroline Carmichael. The scores are low-normal; they make it clear that the clever "Caroline" who engineered Hilary's escape—and Winston's escape—from the Carmichael prison must have been someone other than Caroline Adkins Carmichael. The rest of the chapter explains how the impostor, nurse Martha Sedgewick, succeeded in establishing herself as Caroline.

In the last chapter (13), Winston and Hilary discuss Martha Sedgewick's imposture and how much they owe to it. Winston then picks up the test scores and the other documents that establish the facts of "Caroline's" identity. He plans to go to the funeral home where her body lies and place the documents in the coffin with her. Her imposture will not be made public. Hilary says she will go with him; the two set out to "bury Caroline, and Martha Sedgewick with her" (*F*, 118).

The Characters

The characterization in *Daughter*, like the plot, is more complex than in Konigsburg's earlier books. The reason is the same as for the plot: the chief characters act on two levels, present and past, just as the plot does.

Winston is one of the two-level actors; we soon realize that "she" is also a two-level actor but are unsure of the identity of "she." Winston appears in the italicized passages as an adult. The adult Winston of the present time characterizes himself as reluctant to write, but finally willing. He is ruefully aware of his own limitations: "I'm bound to give myself all the good lines" (*F*, 3). Though he is biddable—he quickly agrees to do what "she" asks and compose this account—he is also assertive: when "she" suggests, "A mood can be an incident," he responds, "Oh, no! . . . No, no, no, no, no. Moods are colors" (*F*, 3). He possesses, moreover, a considerable store of self-knowledge.

This knowledge of self allows Winston to report his earlier jealousy of his sister's involvement with Caroline and his recognition that, concerning Heidi/Hilary, "What cowards we were . . . except you," to which she adds, "And [Caroline]" (*F*, 89). The cowardliness consisted, Winston realizes, in not facing up to Hilary's handicaps and trying to help her overcome them.

The Winston-narrator, in short—the adult Winston of the book's present—is intelligent, self-aware, integrated. At the same time that he characterizes himself in the italicized passages, his narration characterizes the Winston of 24 and 23 years ago as an intelligent but nonintegrated seventh- and eighth-grader.

The 13- or 14-year-old Winston first and last cares for Heidi. Young Winston has other characteristics, to be sure, but his relationship with Heidi colors all those other parts of his character. Konigsburg establishes that relationship in the first chapter. The day that occupies the chapter is Thursday, a "particular wart in [Winston's] week" because on that day it is his responsibility "to amuse Heidi" (*F*, 4).

On all Thursdays, as on this specific Thursday, Heidi asks Winston, "What'll we do today, Winston?" Today he first suggests—with a quiet intensity of feeling—that she ask the cook to teach her to do "two things at once. . . . Like putting your head in the oven and turning on the gas" (*F*, 5). Because Heidi only reads lips and cannot hear, she misses this suggestion. Much of Winston's character is now established; he must amuse his sister, he feels negative toward her, and he is, if not yet shown to be witty, certainly a smart aleck.

To offset this negative first impression is the fact that Winston is also perceptive of Heidi's wants and needs. He—and only he—plays the Invisible Game with Heidi. It consists of identifying items by touch while one is blindfolded. Heidi likes this game because Winston blindfolded is her equal: both are deprived of one sense. Perceptive of Heidi's wishes as he is, though, Winston breaks the chief rule of the game and rips off his blindfold to answer the ringing doorbell, which enrages Heidi.

In short, chapter 1 establishes Winston as Heidi's caretaker, and as a caretaker who, if sensitive to Heidi's needs, also feels considerable animosity toward her. Konigsburg later reveals the depth of this animosity, as when we learn that Winston has a special, secret vocabulary for Heidi and her characteristics. He describes her smile as a "warm, wet, creature smile" (*F*, 6) and her moving as "larruping," like a hyena. Further, he refers to her as a "lower form of life, something cenazoic" (*F*, 35). Later, jealous of Caroline's attention to Heidi's reading, he screams "Chimpanzee" at Heidi (*F*, 63) and thinks to himself that "some hidden part of me" wants Heidi "to always be the golliwog" (*F*, 65). He rages so at a later instance of Caroline's giving attention to Heidi that Caroline can hardly calm him.

The above makes it appear that Winston "cares for" Heidi only in the most mechanical way—as a caretaker at a zoo might care for monkeys to whom he was allergic. That impression is false; Winston does not merely resent Heidi. He is also a loving brother. His real affection for Heidi appears as the two attend a party celebrating Caroline's return. Winston has a good time until he walks over to Heidi, who greets him "with that sad flaying of her arms" (*F*, 59). He sits next to her, and she smiles at him: "It was a hesitant smile, as alone on her face as her person was in the room" (*F*, 60). Winston thinks to himself, "Some part of her knows," and he can't bear it. He hastens from the room, fetches the copy of the Rubaiyat that he bought for Caroline, and gives it to Heidi—to whom we now realize he gives first priority in his feelings.

Winston loves, and sometimes hates, his sister. That seems a normal sibling attitude, though here complicated by Heidi's handicap and Winston's forced caretakership. That he can fulfill the enforced role and nonetheless love his sister shows profound strength of character.

Winston is also presented as imprisoned—imprisoned not only by his enforced labors of love for Heidi but also by his parents' protectiveness. Winston's parents, moved by Caroline's kidnapping years ago, smother him in protection, and he knows it, pointing out to his father that he and Heidi are so much chauffeured and chaperoned that only an act of "an angry God" (*F*, 18) or their own choice could get either of them kidnapped.

The youthful Winston knows he is imprisoned in the Carmichael residence; he does not at first realize he is also imprisoned in his resentful but genuine love of Heidi, which keeps him tied to her. Caroline, though, realizes that Winston feels "responsible" (*F*, 56) for Heidi; this sense of responsibility is part of his "cage" (*F*, 57). To leave his prison, he will have to cease feeling responsible for Heidi, which to Caroline means that she will have to make Heidi independent.

Finally, and by this time obviously, Winston is characterized as loving Caroline, at first as a sister. Later he comes to doubt she is his sister, but he refuses to act on that doubt for 23 years. At the last, when he knows she is not Caroline, he nonetheless sets out with Hilary to go to the funeral parlor where "Caroline's" body awaits burial. Winston, calling her "my other sister" (*F*, 118), plans to bury with her the secret of her identity.

Whereas the characterization of Winston, who is both narrator and protagonist of *Daughter*, is, as one would expect, the book's most extensive, Heidi/Hilary may be the most intense character. She is surely Konigsburg's most complex character to date. We meet her in the initial italicized passage but don't yet know her to be the "she" we presume to be the "arcane daughter" of the title. When we meet Heidi in chapter 1 we decide—consciously or not—that Heidi is not "she." "She" carries on an unimpeded conversation in the italicized paragraphs; Heidi, by contrast, cannot hear. Heidi misses much of a conversation even though she reads lips.

As the book progresses, though, we see Heidi become an intelligent, increasingly self-assured person. Then, thanks to Caroline, Heidi becomes "Hilary"—a Hilary who recognizes her handicaps and works to overcome them. (Caroline, incidentally, is the first to note that using "Heidi" instead of her real name is a way of denying Hilary's handicaps.)

At the close of the book we realize that the italicized "she," the "arcane daughter," is Hilary (now wearing a hearing aid). We also realize that, as the jacket illustration suggests, Hilary has come into view only panel by panel. Moreover, readers will have assumed for much of the book that "she" is Caroline, the only articulate "daughter" we see at first.

Konigsburg accomplishes Hilary's complex characterization, as she did Winston's, by juxtaposing the two plot levels of italicized present-time passages and flashback passages. She also gains depth for Hilary's eventual assumption of the "she" role by making "she" a forceful character. But the center of Hilary's characterization appears in her interaction with Winston. In fact, we never see Heidi/Hilary except through Winston's eyes.

Winston's eyes first show Heidi as the sole element in making Thursday his worst day of the week. Just four pages into the book we see Heidi as abnormal—subnormal, in fact—presented to us by Winston as a creature. This impression grows when, just a page later, Winston breaks the central rule of the Invisible Game and takes off his blindfold. Heidi screams, flattens herself on the floor, and bites Winston's ankle.

The animal imagery, and the nonhuman behavior, continue. It is eventually Caroline who begins to prompt Heidi to "[try] out normalcy" (F, 65) as she insists Heidi be included in the interactions Winston and Caroline enjoy. Heidi becomes "a quiet listener, more a mascot than a pest" (F, 65), though she is still referred to by the animal term "mascot." Hereafter Caroline initiates psychological testing of Heidi that at first frightens Heidi but assures her that she is a genius. Heidi becomes, as Winston observes, "more self-contained" (F, 79), less dependent, as a result.

The climax of this Caroline-inspired change occurs just after Heidi has been forbidden to visit Caroline. Heidi nonetheless persuades Winston to take her to Caroline's apartment, where she and Winston confer with Caroline and the psychologist who has been testing Heidi. Heidi learns that she must decide whether to retreat into her "Heidi" character or to work to accommodate herself to her handicaps and become "Hilary."

That Hilary made the latter decision becomes evident just two pages later, where—as the book settles into its present time, with no more italicized passages—Winston notes that "she" has a walk that is "smooth and heel-toe" and that "only a brother could recognize some vestige of the galumphing golliwog" (F, 100). "She" is Hilary; Heidi no longer exists.

Hilary has a large desk, an array of buzzers, and "special phone sets" (F, 61); her office is on "the executive floor" (F, 61). We eventually learn that she has taken over directing Mr. Carmichael's business after his death. Hilary is the "arcane daughter" (F, 118), says Winston; mysterious to us from the first, she has now come slowly into a reader's view as an independent, capable woman. She has also come into view for Winston as independent and capable; it is a triumph for Konigsburg that a reader's changing view of Hilary parallels the youthful Winston's change.

Central to that change has been Caroline, who enters *Daughter* quietly enough: Konigsburg focuses events on Winston and Heidi as Caroline comes to the Carmichael home. In fact, we only notice her as a catalyst—her ringing the doorbell causes Winston to break the cardinal rule of the Invisible Game, and that in turn causes Heidi to bite him.

Caroline continues her catalytic role throughout the book. Through her influence Winston discovers a "new world" of thoughts, history, geography, and books—especially books. Winston says of Caroline that she "was the first person I had ever known who had read deeply and seriously out of interest and enthusiasm and not simply to pass a test" (*F*, 45).

We learn this about Caroline, and learn in addition that Winston's mother doubts Caroline's identity. Winston himself, in fact, has doubts: "Heidi was made of Carmichael stuff, and Caroline was . . . was what? Caroline was supposed to be Carmichael stuff, too. But I wondered" (*F*, 88). From the first, in fact, Caroline's true identity is a question. She is, then, a mysterious figure through much of the book. This air of mystery leads us to assume that Caroline is the "arcane daughter."

Caroline fosters the mystery in her own right. When Winston tells her she is not Mr. Carmichael's daughter, she neither confirms nor denies the implied charge. She simply gives Winston the envelope, and tells him "I'm tired of all the pretense. Yours and your mother's and your father's. Mine, too" (*F*, 95). She tells him he should do whatever he likes with the envelope and to "decide whether it is more important to know for sure who I am or whether it is enough to know what I am" (*F*, 95). By this point in the story the reader is unsure: Is she the lost daughter? She doesn't seem a fortune hunter, but she doesn't seem a Carmichael either.

The last 18 pages of *Daughter* resolve the identity issue. The real Caroline's intelligence test scores from the envelope report low-normal intelligence, whereas the new Caroline regularly shows well-above-normal intelligence. The penultimate chapter solves the mystery: "Caroline" was Martha Sedgewick, a nurse at the nursing home where Flora Adkins, the mother of Mr. Carmichael's first wife, spent her last months. Mrs. Adkins dis-

liked the new Mrs. Carmichael and did not wish her to inherit
the Adkins fortune. If Caroline reappeared, she would inherit
the fortune. So Flora had briefed Martha—who greatly
resembled Caroline Carmichael—for an impersonation.

And the book is the story of Martha Sedgewick's impersonation, and of its results. As Caroline she freed both Winston and
Heidi/Hilary from the Carmichael prisons—the prisons of
Heidi's denied (and therefore untreated) handicaps and of Winston's tie to Heidi, which prevented his leaving prison on his
own. Impressed with Winston's intelligence, and learning of
Heidi's intelligence, "Caroline" acted as a catalyst for the necessary changes that freed the two children from the weight of their
pasts.

By the time we learn that "Caroline" is an impostor, though,
we know her as intelligent, benevolent, and loving. The strength
of Konigsburg's characterization of "Caroline" appears in this:
though the issue of ill-gotten gains does appear, both "Caroline"
and the reader dismiss it. Instead, we accept Martha's initial
decision to become "Caroline" as prompted by her compassion
first for Flora Adkins, then for Mr. Carmichael, and we accept
her continuing deception as based on her love for Winston and
Heidi.

Style

Konigsburg's typical clever style appears in *Daughter*, usually
through Winston. Winston is witty in both his speech as a youth
and his narrative interjections as the book's adult teller/
composer. His youthful wit appears as he makes mildly off-color
jokes about farts and hickeys, refers to "snot" and "camel-snot"
(*F*, 74, 83), and queries his social studies teacher about Ben
Franklin's common-law wife and "natural" child.

Winston's wit as narrator is considerably more subtle. A
mordant example appears as part of his account of that first
Thursday. Heidi has just called her mother "Mummy," and Winston asks, "Why don't you call our mother, 'Mother'? A mummy
is something all stiff and wrapped in bandages" (*F*, 5). Three
pages later their mother returns home wearing a scarf tied
tightly under her chin. Heidi climbs into her lap and struggles to
untie the stubborn knot of the scarf: "Heidi's fingers tugged and

pulled. Mother sat there, wearing a smile like a cosmetic, as Heidi unwrapped her Mummy" (*F*, 9). The pun on "Mummy" presages the stiffness, even the deadness, that characterize Grace Carmichael throughout *Daughter*.

With its metafictional structure, *Daughter* is Konigsburg's most technically complex book. Its opening passage begins and ends with "she" urging the narrative "I" to "tell it," even though "I" protests that "there are some parts that I hardly know and other parts that I don't know at all," which shows us that this narrator is not omniscient but bound by personal experience. The "I" then says, "For me it all began on a Thursday, a September Thursday in 1952," to which "she" responds, "Begin it there" (*F*, 4).

This opening not only establishes the narrator's viewpoint but also begins the metafictive process: we understand the immediate flashback to a particular Thursday in September 1952 as the beginning of the narrator's obeying the "she" and beginning to "tell it." The narrator self-consciously creates the story before our eyes. That act of creation comes to the fore in the italicized passages, which typically open with questions or observations that shape the nonitalicized, past-time, remainder of the unfolding narrative. This pattern culminates in the last italicized passage, where "she" asks, "Do you still have the envelope?" (*F*, 93). The question brings the book up to its present time.

Konigsburg has carefully joined that present time to the metafictive process. She gives readers enough specific dates —like September 1952—so they can determine the year of the book's "composition" by Winston. This appears late in the book where Winston says he has had the envelope he got from Caroline (in the second week after Easter 1953) for 23 years. Twenty-four years have passed, then, since the story began in September 1952. That makes the book's present time 1976, the year of *Daughter*'s copyright.

This ingenious device gives the book an immediacy that informs its plot even for readers who miss the precise dating of the action. The immediacy is self-conscious too—or "metafictive" again. From the first italicized passage, Winston and "she" have referred to the developing narrative as a "comic strip" wherein

Winston's "telling will be a string of incidents. Like the separate frames of a comic strip" (*F*, 3).

This self-conscious "here we go on another separate frame" approach reflects the book jacket, which *is* a series of separate frames. Moreover, the "comic strip" motif appears in many italicized passages and on the book's last page. In that passage two "fictions" find resolution at once: we learn that "Caroline" is dead and that the envelope holding the secrets of her identity will be buried with her body. As Winston puts it, "She deserves to be buried with some funny papers, the final frames of our comic strip" (*F*, 118). Because the contents of the envelope have been the focus of most of the penultimate chapter, they do include the "final frames" of the comic strip that has become *Father's Arcane Daughter* before our eyes. The metafictive "comic strip" has been prominent throughout the book; we have watched Winston create it, frame by frame.

Themes

The question of identity, again, is *Daughter's* major theme, illustrated most prominently by the fact that, from the first few pages—which identify Winston but leave us mystified as to the identity of "she"—up to page 97, we do not know that the increasingly prominent "she" is Hilary. Nor do we know the identity of the title's "arcane daughter," though we suppose it must be "she." At first we assume "she" to be Caroline, but a clause on page 97 hints otherwise: "She put on an old Heidi pout." Two pages later we learn that "she" is Hilary.

The uncertainty of the identity of "she" has set the tone for a series of identity questions. For one, "Heidi," we recall, is not Hilary's name; it is, Caroline suggests, a way of disguising Hilary's real identity as a person with serious handicaps. And Caroline, of course, poses what at first reading seems the most obvious identity issue: Is she Caroline or an impostor?

That central question Caroline articulates toward the book's close as she hands Winston the envelope holding one answer to the identity question. He may open it if he wishes, she says. He must "decide whether it is more important to know for sure who I am or whether it is enough to know what I am" (*F*, 95). Hence the book's chief theme: identity is not *who* you are but *what* you are. Winston recognizes that fact: he does not open the envelope. Caroline recognizes it too: she sees the sensitive intelligence below Heidi's animal-like exterior. The book closes by affirming this thematic point: Caroline is not "Martha Sedgewick" but "my other sister" (*F*, 118). It is what you do, not who you are, that defines your self. Either is a "truth"; like Winston, one must choose "which truth . . . you want to live with" (*F*, 98).

Identity is not the only theme. Many will find in the Heidi/Hilary characterization the theme of becoming an independent person in spite of physical handicaps. Moreover, Winston's responses to Heidi/Hilary illustrate another theme: sibling love. Although Winston does not seem loving to Heidi as the book opens, nor she to him (remember the bitten ankle), he does care, as is revealed in his giving her Caroline's Rubaiyat. It is a tribute to Konigsburg's uncompromising honesty that the relationship does not become saccharine after that event. Instead, Winston shows a virulent jealousy when Caroline is impressed with Heidi's reading that same Rubaiyat. Even given Winston's jealousy, he and Heidi are bonded profoundly; neither can escape the "Carmichael prison" without the other, as Caroline notes.

Comparable Fiction

Father's Arcane Daughter is a tour de force. The flashback technique appeared earlier, in *A Proud Taste for Scarlet and Miniver*, but here Konigsburg uses it not only to further her plot but also to establish character and theme, and even to make a statement about fiction. A writer works from "a lot of not knowing" (*F*, 3, 118), Hilary suggests. The process of writing, or at any rate of narrating, this book suggests as much. Hilary, prompting the narrator in the italicized chapter openings, shows a reader the seemingly random approach by which frame after frame of the novel comes into view as Winston explores his "not knowing" in "a string of incidents" (*F*, 3). Konigsburg has written no other fiction like this.

Nor has anyone else. No other children's book compares closely, though a few share some of *Daughter*'s themes or points of characterization. Themes of overcoming handicaps appear these days with increasing frequency, in books like Ivan

Southall's *Let the Balloon Go* (1985), in which a cerebral-palsied boy refuses to let his mother define him by what he cannot do but instead tries to do what other boys do (including successfully scaling a tree), and also Barbara Corcoran's *A Dance to Still Music* (1974), in which a girl learns to accept, then cope with, deafness—in spite of her mother. (Mothers get a bad press in these books, it would seem.)

The theme of sibling love, as I have noted, is common to many of Konigsburg's books, and in fact to many modern children's books. Cynthia Voigt's Tillerman family comes to mind. Dicey (in *Homecoming, Dicey's Song,* or even *Seventeen against the Dealer*) is as loving a sister as Winston is a brother; her relationship with the "slow" Maybeth, and her brothers' equally loving relationships with Maybeth, are similar to but less intense than the Winston-Heidi relationship. Loving siblings also appear in Betsy Byars's *The Summer of the Swans*, Ouida Sebestyen's *Words by Heart*, Vera and Bill Cleaver's *Where the Lilies Bloom* and *Trial Valley*, Margaret Mahy's *The Haunting*, and a hearteningly large group of other works.

As with *Dragon*, the parents in *Daughter* leave much to be desired. Upper class rather than upper middle, they if anything imprison their children more tightly than the Foxmeadow ghetto could ever manage. They do not abandon their children, as Jeff's mother abandons him in Voigt's *A Solitary Blue* (1983), but they suffocate them.

7

Finding Yourself—and Someone Else

In *Journey to an 800 Number* (1982) 12-year-old Max (nicknamed "Bo") spends much of his time identifying himself by putting on his heavy blue prep-school blazer with the Fortnum School crest. His journey shows him other ways to establish identity. In *Up from Jericho Tel* (1986) Jeanmarie Troxell also makes journeys, but she does so invisibly. Seeking fame, she discovers that generosity is one of fame's essential elements. She also discovers Malcolm Soo.

Journey to an 800 Number

The action of *Journey* begins with Bo, the narrator, refusing to let his (divorced) father carry Bo's luggage after Bo's arrival at the airport to begin a month-long stay. The book ends a month later with Bo moving luggage out from between them on the car seat in order to sit closer so his father can hug him. Major changes take place between the two events: Bo becomes less of a smart aleck, meets some fascinating people, learns to love his father, and—most important—begins to see his true identity.

The Plot

Various journeys structure the plot of *Journey*. As the story opens, protagonist and narrator Rainbow Maximilian Stubbs

("Bo" as a child—now known as "Max"), is about to fly from Pennsylvania to Texas to join his divorced father for a month while his just-remarried mother, Sarah, honeymoons. Bo's father, Woodrow "Woody" Stubbs, is a camel driver—that is, he travels about and sells rides on his camel, Ahmed. So Bo perforce travels with Woody for the month of his visit.

Bo's travels begin in "Smilax," Texas, where Bo comes down with the flu. For two days Woody nurses him while Bo recovers. The two then journey to Dallas, where Woody and Ahmed are engaged to serve as decorations for a "Mideast Airlines" booth during a convention of travel agents.

On the road to Dallas they meet at a café Sabrina and Lilly—a fifth-grade girl and her mother, respectively. Later, settled into their "gig" at the Dallas Convention Center, Bo and Woody again meet the two; Lilly is registering as a travel agent at the convention for which Ahmed serves as scenery. She is straightening out some confusion about her registration as Woody and Bo re-encounter her and Sabrina and learn that their last name is Pacsek. The four visit off and on through the next several days, and Bo becomes interested in Sabrina.

When the convention ends Bo and Woody travel to Tulsa for the state fair. There Bo meets a Hispanic American family who come to the Tulsa fair each summer, as does Woody. They and Woody are friends. The friendship stands both Woody and Bo in good stead as Woody falls ill with Bo's flu; Manuelo, the eldest boy in the Hispanic American family, takes over running the camel ride while the others help Woody in various ways. Bo—to his lasting regret—questions the correctness of the amount of the camel-ride money Manuelo gives him the first night. Manuelo explains that a customer worked a short-change complaint on him, but he is offended.

Bruised by his recognition that he has been hateful to Manuelo, Bo is glad to leave Tulsa behind following Woody's recovery. He has had four healthful experiences there: he learned his cleverness could make him hate himself (the Manuelo situation), he cared for Woody while Woody was helpless, he saw disinterested friendship in action, and, on the last day of the fair, he entered into an agreement with Woody that for the rest of his month's visit he will comport himself like a polite foreigner in Woody's life, observing with interest the customs strange to him.

From Tulsa, Woody and Bo (and Ahmed) go to Colorado, to a dude ranch outside Denver. There Woody again sells camel rides to visiting conventioneers, and in addition spends every night with Ruthie Britten, a school librarian who works at the ranch each summer. Among the conventioneers frequenting the dude ranch appear Lilly and Sabrina, this time with the last name "Walker." Sabrina explains to Bo that Lilly has taken back her maiden name. During the remainder of his 10 days at the dude ranch, Bo thinks often of Sabrina, concluding that he likes her.

The camel cavalcade's next stop is Las Vegas, where Ahmed is to appear in a stage show in which the lead singer will sit on him while she sings. The lead singer is the English Trina Rose, an old friend of Woody's and—to Bo's amazement—of Bo's mother. Trina, in fact, is Bo's godmother. The upshot of their meeting is that Woody allows Bo to accept Trina's invitation to move into her penthouse suite with her for the remainder of their Las Vegas time. Bo is ecstatic; he likes luxury.

While luxuriating with Trina Rose, Bo learns some of his mother's early life. Trina had driven with "Sally Ghost" (Bo's mother's hippie name) to Woody's home in Taos, New Mexico. The two young women had been hippies together, and used Woody's home as a "crash pad." Bo also learns, from Woody, that Sally Ghost had been pregnant when she and Woody married. Bo is surprised, but not shocked: "I've joined the crowd," he observes, suggesting that half the "first-borns" at his prep school were likewise "pre-expected."[1]

Midway through the stay with Trina, Bo is breakfasting in the hotel restaurant when Sabrina enters, again attending a convention with her mother. Bo's cleverness finally unravels what had bothered him earlier about the nonstop convention-eering of the two: he tells Sabrina that he knows now that she and her mother attend conventions of organizations they don't belong to, then leave the convention hotels without paying for room or meals. Sabrina admits the charge. Lilly, Sabrina tells Bo, is an 800-number telephone answerer—one of the most anonymous jobs Sabrina knows. Beginning by accident, and continuing partly as a reaction against her anonymity, Lilly has for three years adopted different identities and gone to conventions to employ the new identities.

Prompted by this conversation to ponder his own identity, Bo soon asks Trina Rose to tell him more about his mother—about his identity. Trina tells him of Woody's early-apparent love for "Sally Ghost," to which Bo responds, "I know about them." Asked what he knows, Bo replies he knows "Sally" was pregnant with him when she and Woody married. Trina assumes that Woody has now told Bo all the circumstances of his birth, and says Woody has always loved Bo "like you was his very own" (*J*, 135). Questioning this, Bo learns that Sally was indeed pregnant with Bo when she married Woody—but that Woody was not the father.

Now Bo is shocked. Recovering as soon as possible from this disclosure, he asks Trina who his father is. She replies, "Why, I'd say Woody is. Wouldn't you, Love?" (*J*, 136). Bo asks nothing more. For the remaining three days of his month with Woody Bo decides not to bother Woody with questions: he will ask the questions of his mother when he returns to Pennsylvania. In the mean time, he resolves to "just enjoy being his son, Bo" (*J*, 136).

As the father and son drive to the airport on Bo's last day, Bo shifts his blazer off his lap and away from Woody, and moves closer to Woody. The two drive off to the airport, hugging each other.

The Characters

The most fully developed character in *Journey* is the narrator, Bo. Even the name "Bo" is part of Konigsburg's characterization: the narrator begins the book saying that he is no longer the "Bo" of his early (predivorce) life but that he and his mother now "called ourselves Sarah J. (her) and Maximilian R. (me)" (*J*, 6). He has rejected his childhood name and taken the more dignified "Maximilian." In fact, his first words to Woody at the Texas airport are "I'm called Maximilian now" (*J*, 10).

He continues to insist on being called Max, or Maximilian, for much of the early two-thirds of the book. Eventually, though, he discovers that he "really didn't mind being called Bo" (*J*, 79); from then on Woody calls him "Bo" almost exclusively. Once Trina Rose enters the plot, he is exclusively "Bo," except to Sabrina, who has met him as "Maximilian" and continues to call him that name or "Max."

Konigsburg implies much of the narrator's characterization by the first-name confusion. Early in the book Bo tries to be "R. Maximilian," a prep-school youth whose mother has just married someone named F. Hugo Malatesta. As he returns to his father and to the way of life he and his mother shared with his father during his childhood, he increasingly reverts to "Bo." By the time he discovers that Woody has taken him on as Woody's own child, but that he is *not* Woody's biological child, he is solidly "Bo."

Bo/Max has reason for his ambivalence about his first name: when Bo was four his parents divorced and he went east with Sally/Sarah. He seldom saw Woody. Bo likes his mother's choice of life-style. He says, "We developed quite a nice life for ourselves" (*J*, 5) after his mother took the job of "executive housekeeper" at Fortnum School. His upscale concerns first appear in his anxiously assuring the reader that "she didn't actually clean the rooms or cook the food; she supervised the people who did" (*J*, 6). And as has already been noted, their names moved upscale too—and "Sarah J." and "Maximilian R." go well with "F. Hugo Malatesta," the Fortnum School Board of Trustees member whom Sarah marries. Her son is happy with his mother's marriage. He will later report that "I have spent all my time that I can remember trying not to be strange" (*J*, 102), and he embraces every conventional act of his mother's.

Bo's upscale desires also surface when he learns he is to stay with "my father, the camel-keeper" for the month of his newly-wed mother's honeymoon. Bo persuades her to get him his Fortnum School blazer before he goes to join Woody, and, despite the intense heat and humidity of a Texas August, he gets off the plane wearing the blazer. He insists on wearing it all day (until Woody leaves to take Ahmed to the local shopping mall), wishing nothing to come between him and the preppie, conventional way of life his mother has chosen for them.

Bo's estrangement from Woody remains central to his actions during the first two-thirds of the book. He barely greets Woody at the airport, and accepts no help with his luggage. Later, when they arrive at Woody's trailer, Bo refuses to go see

Ahmed, saying he has some letters he wants to write. All told, he could hardly have made a more forbidding first impression on his host and father.

This estranged prickliness continues through Woody's nursing Bo through an influenza attack and back to health. The attitude is not proof, however, against the next event: Bo takes over and nurses Woody back to health after Woody comes down with Bo's flu as the two arrive at the Tulsa state fair. Bo cares for Woody devotedly for several days and thereafter agrees to comport himself as a polite "foreigner" while visiting Woody and Ahmed: he will observe the customs but will not try to change them. From this point on Bo mellows. He even speaks of Woody to Sabrina with definite respect.

Another aspect of Bo's characterization is his sardonic sense of humor. It first appears shortly after the book opens, as Bo explains his name: he says that Woody had promised Bo's mother to "name me according to an old Indian custom"—that is, to name him for "the first thing he saw" outside the hospital of Bo's birth. Led blindfolded outside, then un-blindfolded, "the first thing my father saw was a rainbow. . . . My real name is Rainbow Maximilian Stubbs" (*J*, 6). Bo adds, "Both my parents always regarded it as a good omen that the first thing that Father saw after I was born was a rainbow. So do I. After all, there was a chance that I could have been called One Dog Squatting" (*J*, 7).

The chief thrust of Konigsburg's characterization of Bo is his search to find his identity. As the book opens he is satisfied to use his Fortnum School blazer to proclaim who and what he is. So much has he identified himself with the blazer, in fact, that after a fracas with some youths while washing Ahmed at a car wash he takes off his camel-washing clothes, puts on his blue blazer, and only then begins "to feel a little more like myself" (*J*, 44). The blazer continues to be Bo's armor: he wears it during his last meal with Sabrina, after which she says, "It's like you have to look at [the blazer's school crest] to know who you are" (*J*, 133).

It is after this challenge that Bo asks Trina Rose to tell him "about when my mother was Sally Ghost" (*J*, 134). From the ensuing conversation he not only learns that Woody is not his biological father but also that Woody, in spite of this, has loved Bo, has put up with his moods throughout this visit, and, as Trina implies, has more right to be called Bo's father than does anyone else. Bo now has a good start toward finding his identity. He says of himself that he *is* himself as Woody's son. He is content to rest in that identity for now. He can put the Fortnum School blazer to one side—it need no longer come between him and his father. He will save his questions for his mother.

Bo (or Max) sounds rather forbidding up to this point, and in fact he often is. Note, though, that Bo is often thoroughly decent. He doesn't allow youths at a car wash to bully Woody, he hates himself for implying that Manuelo cheated Woody of some camel-ride money, and he resolves not to "worry Woody" (*J*, 136) during the last days of his visit. When Bo can step outside his own identity crises, he is pleasant.

A final note in Bo's characterization: he develops a romantic interest in Sabrina during the course of the story, or at least as much of a romantic interest as a 12- or 13-year-old male is likely to develop toward a fifth-grade girl. That interest leads to his wanting to impress her. Thus he wears his blazer whenever he knows he'll see her and he brags to her of his "going to go to Fortnum School in the fall. That's a private school. College prep" (*J*, 37). His bragging to her, in fact, leads the clear-seeing Sabrina to suggest that he is finding his identity in his blazer.

Sabrina's role in *Journey* is smaller than Bo's. She appears early in the book, and favorably impresses "Maximilian" (as Bo then wishes to be called). He and Woody enter into conversation with Sabrina and her mother, Lilly; following this conversation, Bo records his impression of Sabrina as "going-on-pretty" —except for her eyes, which "were already pretty. Maybe beautiful" (*J*, 30). He adds that her nose, mouth, smile, and teeth are all pretty too.

Like Bo, Sabrina is a child of divorced parents and is lively in conversation. When she tells Bo that she and Lilly went by the El Al (Israeli Airlines) booth and had chicken soup for lunch, Bo asks,

"How was it? Was it gourmet?"
"It was authentic."

"But was it gourmet?"

"If chicken soup is gourmet, it's not authentic. Did you know that a recent study showed that chicken soup is good for the common cold?"

"Even if you're not Jewish?"

"Even if you don't have a cold." (*J*, 50–51)

Like Bo, Sabrina is quick—and in this exchange even quicker. She continues to be quicker than Bo throughout the book. Bo is intrigued, and we see considerable interest on his part as Sabrina becomes established as a knowing person.

To be sure, Sabrina is only 10, but when she says her "chronological age is . . . merely one of my disguises" (*J*, 99), we are likely to believe her. She particularly impresses Bo through her comments on pretending. She tells him everyone wants, even needs, to pretend sometimes. Normal people can decide "whether or not we want to present ourselves or present a disguise" (*J*, 98). Bo does not yet see his Fortnum School blazer as such a disguise, but both the reader and Sabrina do. "It's you, Maximilian Stubbs, who doesn't know who you are" (*J*, 133), she tells Bo. She then makes her comment on his HELLO badge.

A particular strength of Woody's characterization is that much of it comes through his silences. When Bo cracks wise at him, or says something cruelly tactless, Woody responds with silence or a jocular remark that refuses to meet Bo's statement. For example, when Bo "greets" Woody with complaints about airline food at the airport at Smilax, Woody just "studied" (*J*, 11) him a bit longer, then put his arm around Bo and went with him to get the luggage. Bo had just coldly informed Woody, "I'm called Maximilian now," to which Woody makes no comment but simply begins calling Bo "Max" and introduces him to others as "my son, Maximilian" (*J*, 30). He does not again call him "Bo" until after Bo has nursed Woody through his illness—at which point Bo discovers he doesn't mind it at all.

As Bo finds out when Woody becomes ill in Tulsa, everyone likes Woody. People bring gifts and show their concern, and the Hispanic American family runs the camel ride and helps Bo. That everyone loves Woody is not surprising: he seems quietly interested in everyone (as he shows when he first converses with

Sabrina and her mother) and rejects no one.

That Woody rejects no one becomes a major virtue when he talks to Bo about Bo's mother without being in any way censorious or judgmental. "I didn't ask questions" (*J*, 120), he says of his association with Bo's mother, and Bo observes that Woody does not question people. He does not question; he does not reject. Woody has not rejected Bo, and that is perhaps the major part of his characterization. He has had reason to find Bo rejectable, but he has been loving instead. The chief example of his loving nature appears when Bo asks why his mother's parents rejected her. Woody admits to Bo that his mother "was pregnant when we got married" (*J*, 120), but never suggests that anyone but he himself was Bo's father. He did not reject the pregnant Sally, and he does not reject the child of another man who was born to the Sally who divorced him.

Another major character in *Journey* does not appear until the last 32 pages. Trina Rose, the English singer whom Bo and Woody join in Las Vegas, is unlike any character Konigsburg has developed. Trina was one of the young people who lived at Woody's home outside Taos during the years he maintained a "crash pad" there. Named Caterina Rosenblum but known then as "Baby Bloom," she arrived at Woody's ranch with "Sally Ghost," Bo's mother. Sally, and soon Woody, were her very good friends. Trina, in fact, became Bo's godmother. Leaving the ranch, Trina went on to become a singing star. Remembering Woody and Ahmed, she arranged to have Ahmed engaged for her act in Las Vegas.

Following that necessary exposition (all explained to Bo by Woody), Trina Rose erupts from the pages of the book like a rocket. To both eye and ear she is amazing—perhaps even shocking. She appears monumentally unprepossessing: "Trina Rose was fat . . . fat like a huge scoop of vanilla ice cream that's been at room temperature for a couple of hours. She wore dresses that looked like a parachute with a hole cut in the center for her head and neck. She billowed when she walked" (*J*, 108). Konigsburg's book-jacket drawing of her matches Bo's description.

Trina's first dialogue sets the tone. Becoming aware of Woody waiting off-stage to tell her he and Ahmed have arrived, she runs over to him with arms stretched wide: "Woodrow Stubbs, you bloody old fart.... How's that short-haired, long-legged beast of yours? I'm referring to Ahmed, of course. Nothing private intended" (*J*, 108–9). The loud, earthy tone is marked, and it characterizes Trina for the remainder of the book. She was Bo's "bloody damn godmother" (*J*, 109), she tells him; her speech throughout the remainder of the book is peppered with "bloodies" and "damns"; once she even says, "Balls! Woody[,] I goddam love that kid" (*J*, 119).

If Trina has a surprisingly profane mouth, she also has a surprising large heart. She not only dedicates the first rehearsal of her new show to Bo, but she also invites him to stay with her in her penthouse suite. She is also circumspect. While he stays with her in her suite Bo quizzes her about the Taos days with Woody and his mother: "Although she told me some things, she never told me enough to give me a clear picture of how my tailored mother had once been a girl named Sally Ghost" (*J*, 114). Instead, she leads Bo to tell her of his life, and especially of his past month of life with Woody.

Trina Rose has sound instincts, and she is surprisingly discreet; she tells Bo nothing about his mother except the most general details. Only after Bo reports that Woody has told Bo his mother was pregnant with Bo when the two were married does Trina, perhaps inadvertently, say "He was crazy about that girl, and he loved you like you was his very own" (*J*, 135). When Bo asks Trina Rose, "Who is my father?," she replies with understated profundity, "Why, I'd say Woody is. Wouldn't you, Love?" (*J*, 136).

In a conversation about the unique Trina Rose, Konigsburg said, "I've gotten some questions about Trina's language; when I was writing her, though, those were the words that came naturally to the character" (Interview, January 1989). Konigsburg has no doubt her young readers can deal with Trina's earthiness; adult readers, more prone to hypocrisy, may find problems here.

Style

In *Journey*, as in all her books, Konigsburg's style is a major strength. To be sure, the plot elements of "camel" and "divorce" may first capture the reader's interest (both appear in the first paragraph), but the style of the lively dialogue in the predivorce argument between Woody and Sally sustains that interest. The humor that next appears, in Bo's sardonic comment about his name of "Rainbow Maximilian Stubbs," captivates readers as it sets a standard for the wit and humor throughout *Journey*.

Konigsburg's description of August weather in Texas is a good example of her sardonic humor. She reports the weather through Bo, arriving in Texas on an airplane: "It was the first Saturday in August, and when they . . . opened the door, I thought that someone—God—had made a mistake. There was no out-of-doors there. There was no air there. I felt that I was breathing mayonnaise. I was sweating down to my insteps and up to my eyelids" (*J*, 9–10). This description, certainly Texas-style hyperbole, is very funny.

An example of Konigsburg's style at its best is Bo's response to learning that Woody is not, after all, his biological father: "There was an air space in my throat that swelled like a small balloon, and my heart developed sharp edges and began flipping like a match box bruising me inside. I swallowed that balloon and let it tamp down all the screaming that was inside of me. I did not cry" (*J*, 135–36). Both anatomically and emotionally, this description is precisely right.

A surprising element of Konigsburg's style—and one that also appears in her characterization of Trina Rose—is the book's pronounced earthiness. Trina is the epitome of earthiness, but elsewhere in the book appear numerous terms and situations foreign to most children's books, and heretofore foreign to Konigsburg's books. The "One Dog Squatting" (*J*, 7) line, for instance, begins a strain of bathroom expressions: Woody tells Bo that during his two-day bout of flu he frequently "peed in a bottle" (*J*, 18, 19); one of the smart-aleck youths at the car wash suggests of Ahmed that he needs "no pit stops or shit stops" (*J*, 42); and an elliptical line-vacancy slightly later implies the word "shit" (*J*, 47). Trina Rose's later reference to Sally's new husband as "this F. Hugo Fart" is of a piece both with her characterization and with the monosyllabic earthiness noted above. On a considerably higher plane, but still "earthy" to many readers of children's books, is the incident of Woody's staying several nights with Ruthie Britten while working at the dude ranch near Denver.

Some mild earthiness has figured in Konigsburg's books since Claudia of *Files* directed Jamie to enter the men's room and "stand on it" (i.e., on the toilet). *Journey*, however, with Woody's affair, Trina Rose's language, and the fecal monosyllables, goes much further than do her other works. None of these words are unknown on the elementary- or secondary-school playground, of course; Konigsburg's readers will not learn any new terms here.

We must note, too, that earthiness is appropriate for the book's context. Konigsburg felt that Trina Rose's character required the ribald speech typical of her experiences and vocation; moreover, "shit" is precisely the term one would expect from an adolescent male trying to be impressive at a car wash. The book's language rings true.

Themes

Once again, Konigsburg's major theme in *Journey* is the question of identity—here personified by Bo. He tries to be "as normal as everyone else at Fortnum Preparatory School for Boys" (*J*, 102), he pursues the conventional values represented by "F. Hugo Malatesta the First," and the conventional HELLO badge he presents to the world is his Fortnum blazer. But he seeks further. Thus he asks Woody and Trina questions about his roots; the identity he finds is not what he expected. As the book closes he has chosen one identity—Woody's son—and plans to inquire further. Bo is developing an identity throughout *Journey*, and still doing so as the story ends.

Konigsburg also approaches identity through divorce in *Journey*. The book presents no easy way of coping with divorce; it does suggest that children encounter problems, especially with identity, following a divorce. Konigsburg gives those problems a sympathetic but hard-headed appraisal. Children of divorce will recognize their caught-in-between situation in this book as they see Bo caught between Woody and his mother.

In a final theme, the book suggests that Bo's frantic desire to conform is a mistake. Woody and his way of life appear considerably more attractive than do F. Hugo Malatesta and his life-style. F. Hugo would never have a camel; Woody does. Ahmed the camel is to some degree a metaphor in *Journey*, just as dragons were a metaphor in *Dragon;* Bo seems to need a camel (though he doesn't know it) just as much as Andy Chronister needed a dragon. Seeking conformity has not done much for Bo; early in the book he is a narrow-minded smart aleck, deploring all he sees that does not fit his notion of conventionality. Only later, and especially with Trina Rose, does he accept, even adopt, unconventionality. At that point he learns who he is—or at least he begins to learn who he is.

Comparable Fiction

No children's books are directly comparable to *Journey*: few ex-hippie camel-driver fathers grace the pages of these books. Several, however, address the issues of father-child relationships, and of divorce. Cynthia Voigt's *A Solitary Blue* (1983) deals with both issues, in somewhat the same manner as does *Journey*. Early in the book Jeff's mother, Melody, leaves him and "the Professor," as he calls his father (who *is* a professor). Much of the book deals with Jeff's recovering from her desertion; much of it also deals with Jeff and his father's discovery of one another. Unlike the case in *Journey*, the father is the distant one in *Blue*; only toward the book's close does he unbend to Jeff—much as Bo unbends to Woody—to show Jeff the caring and vulnerable human under the surface of the preoccupied academic. Most children's books about divorce and fathers seem to focus on the father-daughter relationship—for instance, Paula Fox's *The Moonlight Man* (1986), Paul Fleischman's *Rear-View Mirrors* (1986), and Bruce Brooks's *Midnight Hour Encores* (1986).

Up from Jericho Tel

In *Journey* Bo found a father and even a significant other: Sabrina. Jeanmarie Troxell, the narrator of *Tel*, never mentions a father, nor does she seek one. She seeks fame on the stage. She has never told anyone of her dream, however, nor even tried out for a play: "It was as if trying for it would show everyone some secret, hidden part of myself that they could make fun of and hurt."[2] During the course of the book she learns that she must chance being hurt in order to achieve stardom. Having learned that, and considerably more, she wins her first role. She also wins a friend: Malcolm Soo, who, though very different from her (as Sabrina is from Bo), complements her character in important ways.

The Plot

In *Tel* Konigsburg explores a region she lightly touched on once before: fantasy, specifically ghost fantasy. In "Camp Fat" (*Altogether, One at a Time*) she introduced a sympathetic counselor, Miss Natasha, who only appears at night and who, at story's end, proves to have died some years earlier. *Tel*, however, takes a much more thoroughgoing approach to ghostly fantasy.

Jeanmarie Troxell narrates *Tel*. She says in the opening sentence that the events of the book happened when she was 11 years old. She was then in the sixth grade, we later learn, and the dates of the recollected events are "between the start of a new school year and Midwinter's Night" (*U*, 3). The narrator never announces the year of the events but notes that the movie *The Exorcist* has just appeared. That occurred in 1973, so Jeanmarie is presumably looking back to fall 1973.

Jeanmarie and her mother have recently moved from Texas to Long Island. Jeanmarie has become a latchkey kid, spending much of her time unsupervised in their home in a trailer park. Walking from the bus stop to her home after school one day, she finds a dead blue jay. Though fearing to touch it lest she contract some "dread disease," she feels the bird ought to be buried. Another sixth-grader, Malcolm Soo, agrees with her and helps her bury the bird. They make something of a ceremony of the burial.[3] Other burials follow—of a luna moth, a mole, and a baby squirrel. The children choose for their burials a clearing isolated from the rest of the trailer park by a circle of trees. Jeanmarie names the clearing "Jericho Tel" (*U*, 17).

In the process of conducting the burials, and of commemorating the deaths by composing and penning "weathergrams," and hanging them from trees near the new graves, Jeanmarie and Malcolm become friends. ("Weathergrams" are poems of 10 or fewer words written on brown paper and hung on a tree for the weather to dissolve.) The two share their dreams: Malcolm wants to win a Nobel Prize in science; Jeanmarie confides she wants to become a "great actress."

The two children next find a dead dog—a dalmatian. He lies just at the edge of Jericho Tel. As they begin to bury him, both children are sucked down below the surface of the Tel in an experience that one would expect to be terrifying but is instead enjoyable. They come to rest atop a lavender metal box, then fall through it to a doorway. The door leads into a room containing another person: Tallulah.[4] Tallulah has two "assignments" for the children; once they complete these assignments, or tests, successfully, they will be qualified to seek the "Regina Stone," a diamond in a necklace that vanished when Tallulah died of a heart attack 10 years ago. As Tallulah explains, "Someone had robbed her corpse of The Regina Stone" (*U*, 77).

Jeanmarie and Malcolm undertake the two assignments, aided both by instantaneous travel and by Tallulah's making them invisible. They observe a fraudulent healer-evangelist and expose him in a memorable bit of slapstick that includes Malcolm's repeatedly unzipping the fraudulent healer's fly; they later observe, but do not expose, two charming theatrical people bilking an expensive restaurant out of a meal.

Tallulah tells them they have succeeded in their two trials; they learned to tell "the real from the phony" (*U*, 68–69) and to let well enough alone. Having learned those two things, they are ready to seek out the thief of the Regina Stone.

The remainder of the book tells of their search for Tallulah's stolen diamond. Jeanmarie and Malcolm focus their search on the three friends of Tallulah who were present at her death, all of whom were "buskers," street entertainers in New York City. They are

> Emmagene Krebs, a singer who somewhat mystically says she has only 18,000 songs to sing in her life, and who gets her needed "break" but somehow does not catch on.
>
> Nicolai Ion Simonescu, a ventriloquist whose dummy, "Anna Karenina," is popular only with very bright children (he finally stops performing and manufactures puppets instead).
>
> Patrick Henry Mermelstein, a (hopelessly inept) magician who

eventually decides he hasn't the talent to pursue magicianship and opens a magic store instead.

All three have failed in their attempts at stardom. In fact, Simonescu and Mermelstein have turned to other careers, at which they succeed. Emmagene is still busking; she sings at Washington Square in Greenwich Village in New York City. One of the three, the children decide, must have stolen the diamond.

During an invisible visit to the Long Island center for the Internal Revenue Service (where slapstick humor again occurs, with Jeanmarie invisibly tackling various workers, then threatening them with a pen and with animal noises), Malcolm uses a computer to obtain the home addresses for Simonescu and Mermelstein. Jeanmarie visits Simonescu, and both children visit Mermelstein; the upshot of the visits is that the two former buskers agree to perform again at Washington Square on the night of 22 December (Midwinter Night).

Mermelstein and Simonescu meet Emmagene in Washington Square (as Jeanmarie and Malcolm had intended). The three have not seen one another in 10 years; their joyous reunion lasts until the two children appear, introduce the topic of Tallulah, and see Emmagene make a betraying motion toward her throat. Jeanmarie compels her to show the Regina Stone hanging around her neck. She stole it because it was "lucky" for Tallulah, and Emmagene felt that all she needed to succeed was one lucky break; she knew she had talent. But though her break did come, it produced nothing; her one engagement somehow failed to bring others in its wake. And she now has only 542 songs left.

After confessing the theft, Emmagene starts to give the Regina Stone to Jeanmarie. The girl stops her, telling her she will soon meet her self-imposed talent-limit and will then need "to live off what The Regina Stone can bring" (*U*, 174). Emmagene leaves; the two male buskers, considerably sobered, return Jeanmarie and Malcolm to their homes.

The children visit Jericho Tel often thereafter, wanting Tallulah to tell them they responded properly in not reclaiming her Regina Stone. Tallulah never reappears. The book ends with Jeanmarie successfully trying out for, and performing, the title role in her school's play of *Rumpelstiltskin*. She has learned something about stardom; so has Malcolm.

The plot reads something like a mystery—and with a ghost no less. It is a mystery to the two children, and perhaps to young readers on their first reading: Who stole the Regina Stone? Nancy Drew and the Hardy Boys would be comfortable with this question, were it the only question the book asked.

Tel is also a ghost story—after all, Tallulah is a ghost—but one much like "Camp Fat": nonfrightening. Just as Jeanmarie noted concerning her being "sucked down" into Jericho Tel that she should feel frightened but was not, the reader will likewise find in *Tel* none of the frissons that greet, for example, readers of Philippa Pearce's eerie short stories in *Shadow Cage* (1977). Similarly, Tallulah-as-ghost does not frighten either *Tel*'s characters or us. Ghosts in most middle-age-children's books *are* frightening: in Eleanor Cameron's *The Court of the Stone Children* (1973), for example, the heroine feels freezing cold and then faints when she realizes her companion is a ghost. But *Tel* is not that sort of ghost story, just as it is not a standard mystery.

In fact, *Tel* is not primarily mystery or ghost story. Tallulah, the text hints, has known all along who stole her diamond (Why else ascertain early that the two children know to let well enough alone—that is, to leave the Regina Stone with Emmagene?). Retrieving the stolen diamond is not Tallulah's goal. Her goal is to enable the children to find their identities and learn how to be "stars." And that is where the book ultimately finds its center.

The Characters

Jeanmarie Troxell, Malcolm Soo, and Tallulah are the chief characters of *Tel*. Both children are sixth-graders, both are latchkey kids, and both are only children in single-parent families. Both are loners; Jeanmarie rejects the "clones" she sees in her sixth-grade peers, and Malcolm simply ignores them, probably to concentrate on his studies. The two are alike in several important ways, then. Their differences are yet more important, and Tallulah is wildly different from both.

Jeanmarie, an outsider at school, defines herself early as a "future famous person" (*U*, 4) and a "future star of stage, screen,

and TV" (*U*, 10). She also defines herself as having done nothing
to achieve stardom up to this point in her life. Significantly, she
feels she can tell Malcolm her dream of stardom, and does,
which is the first time she has given her desire voice. From this
point on, Konigsburg characterizes her as moving toward stardom. At the same time, Konigsburg characterizes Jeanmarie as
moving from timidity to self-assurance.

Jeanmarie's move to self-assurance develops from her bouts
of invisibility, which give her a sense of freedom, a feeling that
she will "do everything right" (*U*, 51). Her invisible self-posses-
sion proves transferable; visible, at school, and faced with an
officious (and small-minded) office worker, she mendaciously
talks her way around the woman, saying later in some surprise,
"It was as if the invisible part of me made it up" (*U*, 64). Later,
her hair and clothes insulted by two girls who are social leaders
among the "clones," she is able to outface them (literally—she
stares them down).

Tallulah's influence is clearly part of Jeanmarie's increasing
ability to control herself, and therefore others. When chief clone
Lynette Hrivnak, for example, offers her "charity" so Jeanmarie
may attend a performance of the Rockettes at Radio City Music
Hall, Jeanmarie refuses in the sweetest possible tones, saying
among other things, "I have never thought what the Rockettes
do can be called dancing ... darling" (*U*, 116). The "darling" is
Tallulah's characteristic word; Jeanmarie reflects Tallulah's
typically pointed verbal dueling while maintaining her self-
control. That same control appears on the night when Jeanmarie and Malcolm confront the three buskers: "For the first
time ever, my visible self took control of an adult conversation"
(*U*, 170). She controls the conversation to the point where she
can say, "Take off the coat, Emmagene" (*U*, 172); shortly thereafter the Regina Stone appears.

Performance follows self-assurance. Where Jeanmarie had
merely dreamed of being a star earlier (and "never even tried
out for the Fifth Grade Christmas Pageant" [*U*, 15]), she progresses to where she tells not only Malcolm of her dream but
even Tallulah. She moves to performing a poem for a group of
family and friends and eventually tries out for a part in the
sixth-grade play, gets it, and is "wonderful" (*U*, 177–78).

Jeanmarie was a Milquetoast and a nonperformer when she first went to Jericho Tel. She has, indeed, moved "Up from Jericho Tel." Like all of Konigsburg's major characters, she has found her identity. She takes her place alongside Louise Fitzhugh's Harriet Welsch in *Harriet the Spy* (1964) in finding that to fulfill one's promise one must perform. Just as Harriet becomes editor of her class paper and writes stories that people actually read, instead of keeping her writing to herself in her notebook, likewise Jeanmarie goes public with her acting.

Malcolm Soo is also an important character. A major part of Jeanmarie's characterization, in fact, is her growing relationship with Malcolm. The two complement one another: where Jeanmarie is intuitive, dramatic, and excitable, Malcolm is rational, understated, phlegmatic. The contrast appears in their first conversation. Jeanmarie has found the dead blue jay, and Malcolm comes to see what she has found. Jeanmarie says,

> "We ought to keep it from rotting."
> "Everything rots," Malcolm replied.
> "It ought to be buried."
> "It will still rot. It will just rot out of sight." (*U*, 5)

Malcolm is not merely a foil for Jeanmarie, however. Korean and a "half-orphan" (his mother has died), he is an "overachiever" (*U*, 60), as he tells Jeanmarie. He, too, grows during the book's events. Neat, tidy, controlled, and superrational, he comes to learn that reason alone cannot account for everything.

Malcolm's neatness appears from the first: his school-constructed map of the states west of the Mississippi is virtually perfect, and his penmanship looks good on the weathergrams. Moreover, he feels "very much at home" (*U*, 83) with computers and does not forget numbers once he sees them. With such a mind, Malcolm's announcing he dreams of becoming a famous scientist—a Nobel Prize winner, in fact—is no surprise.

Though his tidiness is part of his intellect, Malcolm is almost too tidy; he complains, for example, when the weathergrams don't rhyme. Moreover, when Tallulah fails to send for the children for several days in a row, he tells Jeanmarie both that he "didn't see how being invisible accomplished anything" and that "the facts seem to bear me out" (*U*, 112), perhaps the most infuriating statement a human can utter.

In fact, Malcolm, for the first two-thirds of *Tel*, is fact-bound: he wants to act as if only facts—those things whose existence can be proven scientifically—are real. That changes; after an event he can't explain at his cousins' home, he concludes that "there is a language other than words," which he finds troublesome but undeniable. As he puts it, "I don't like the idea that there's more to life than its facts, but it seems that is a fact of life" (*U*, 142).

Having learned that life is more than its facts, Malcolm is ready to act in the drama Tallulah helps him and Jeanmarie to engineer. He meets with Emmagene and her two old companions, and it is he, not Jeanmarie, who tells Emmagene why she cannot be a star. "You are not generous with your talent," he explains. "You keep track, you have always kept track, and you shouldn't" (*U*, 174). This is not a logical conclusion, but we feel that Malcolm has intuited correctly.

Malcolm, then, recognizes star quality—or lack thereof. He saw its lack in Emmagene. He sees the quality itself in Jeanmarie. Thus not only does he give her a Christmas gift of *A Parliament of Sound: Poems to Read Out Loud*, he ushers her into her first performance: he sets her up to read one of the poems to the assembled family and guests. Like Jeanmarie, Malcolm has added important elements to his identity.

Jeanmarie and Malcolm have already begun to be an "us" when they meet Tallulah, who becomes the catalyst to their further growth. The ghostly actress first appears on Konigsburg's book cover, where she exactly matches Jeanmarie's later description: "a tall, slender woman with long straight red hair—a red that was as natural as lipstick—and a big red mouth (also as natural as lipstick). Her eyes were outlined in black pencil in addition to wearing such heavy false eyelashes that they looked as if she had glued a millipede over each. Her eyes were green. . . . [She] was smoking a cigarette that she held in a long, black cigarette holder" (*U*, 24).[5] Jeanmarie later adds to this description an account of her "low pebbly voice" (*U*, 98).

Tallulah is a star. Adult readers will surmise this from their familiarity with actress Tallulah Bankhead; children learn as much shortly after Tallulah's first appearance, when she mentions the Regina Stone and adds that it was given her "in honor of my most famous role" (*U*, 27). Later she says that she "ruled Broadway" (*U*, 108) when she was alive.

At first, Tallulah's interest in the children seems to be explained by her intent to send them "Topside" (*U*, 77) to undergo certain tests, then find her diamond. Konigsburg's characterization, however, makes it clear that Tallulah has interests in the children beyond their running an errand for her.

Some of that characterization might be described as "makeup"; it establishes Tallulah as Tallulah, a character distinctly different from the two children and distinctly a star. Everything from her being a ghost living underground to her flamboyant star quality to her companion dalmatians make her unique. So do her first words to Jeanmarie after Jeanmarie has sunk into Tallulah's domain: "Close the door before you let all that disgusting fresh air in" (*U*, 24).

That statement sets the tone for Tallulah's language. Jeanmarie presents several of Tallulah's aphorisms as chapter epigraphs: *"Never have a long conversation with anyone who says 'between you and I'"* (*U*, 79) is one example. Other such pithy statements punctuate almost every conversation, as when she tells Jeanmarie not to trouble herself about the "clones" and their jealousy of Jeanmarie's outfit: "Really, darling, don't seek great reviews from small minds. They have neither the character nor the vocabulary for them" (*U*, 107). In short, Tallulah is wildly different from the two children and from the book's child readers, and her differences fascinate.

Tallulah does not enter the story merely to add spark, however; she plays the central role in helping the children discover their identities. She helps Jeanmarie realize that stars must take risks—so Jeanmarie had better risk trying out for a part in the school play or give up her dream: "Wanting is not enough; you must also try. And try out" (*U*, 155). Tallulah also helps Malcolm find out that his approach to science has been too limited—too factual. The following dialogue contributes to Malcolm's realization that "there's more to life than its facts" (*U*, 142) and adds profundity to his dawning understanding of the nature of his world. Tallulah says,

"There is no difference between being an artist and being a scientist.

Malcolm replied, "Yes there is. A scientist is methodical. A scientist thinks logically. . . .

"Well, darling, a true scientist . . . is an artist. . . . Both are seekers of truth. . . . [I]f you are going to be merely logical and merely mechanical, you will never be a star. Just as an actress has to think as well as feel, a scientist must feel as well as think." (*U*, 156–77)[6]

The role of adult opener of doors for child or children has appeared in other children's books: Lena Sills's father, Ben, is an inspiration to her throughout Ouida Sebestyen's *Words by Heart* (1979), and in the book's violent climax Ben is able to teach his daughter a final lesson—to turn the other cheek, even over Ben's death, so that good may come from it. Likewise Josie, an older woman who is a maid in a Florida motel in Barbara Corcoran's *A Dance to Still Music* (1974), is able to calm the newly deaf Margaret and open for her the doors to eventually dealing positively with deafness by going back to school.

Although the helpful adult is not a new character to either Konigsburg (remember Mrs. Frankweiler, Bessie Setzer, Edie Yakots, "Caroline," and Woody) or children's literature in general, Tallulah is distinctive in this role. The only parallel I can think of is the constructively eccentric Merlin in T. H. White's *The Sword in the Stone* (1939).

Style

As the foregoing discussion of Tallulah suggests, Konigsburg again shows her typical stylistic cleverness in *Tel*. That cleverness appears in the idea of the "weathergrams," in several carefully detailed descriptions, and, especially, in Tallulah's dialogue.

"Weathergrams" appear throughout *Tel*. Jeanmarie's best is perhaps the alliterative "*Fly. Flutter. Falter. Fall*" (*U*, 13) for the dead luna moth.

Another constant in Konigsburg's writing is her use of highly specific descriptions. The description of New York City's "buskers," for example, not only establishes the characters of the three "suspects" in the Regina Stone theft but also describes

New York City busker life in loving detail. These numerous descriptive and detailed passages add an air of solid reality to a book whose plot includes a ghost, invisibility, and instantaneous travel.

Though the weathergrams and the descriptive writing are memorable in *Tel*, readers will most clearly remember Tallulah's witty dialogue. When Malcolm has explained chlorophyll and launched into "energy cycles," for example, Tallulah stops him: "Now, now, Malcolm, let's not get carried away. Good explanations are like bathing suits, darling; they are meant to reveal everything by covering only what is necessary" (*U*, 68). See also her response to a leading man who fell in love with her in the part she played opposite him: "I told him that I, Tallulah, was much more than the sum of my parts, and that was far more than he could handle" (*U*, 136).

Themes

By the end of *Tel* Jeanmarie has achieved a major success and appears well on her way to stardom. Malcolm, the text also tells us, has learnt a lesson essential to a budding scientist. Both children have learned—from Tallulah and from their own seeking—the nature of "star quality," whether in the theater or in the laboratory. That quality comprises a trio of characteristics none of the three buskers possesses in full; it also includes a willingness to be vulnerable, and a certain balance.

The trio of characteristics that Malcolm—spurred by Tallulah—concludes make up "star quality" are talent, timing (or "luck" or "getting a break"), and generosity—a generosity that does *not* count its songs but gives all it has. Of the buskers, Simonescu had both talent and generosity but never got the necessary "breaks." Mermelstein the magician, on the other hand, had no talent: breaks would have been wasted on him, and though he had the necessary generosity, it was irrelevant. Emmagene had talent and got a break, but she lacked generosity.

The buskers, then, define "star quality" by what they lack. The text is not contemptuous of them, though; Simonescu succeeds as a manufacturer of puppets, and Mermelstein as a salesman of magic tricks. Emmagene alone does not succeed; she

tried to steal her break. The theft worked, but then, given her
lack of generosity with her talent, she failed. She leaves *Tel* with
her songs numbered: 542 more, then she must stop singing. She
limits herself, and her limits condemn her. A fourth quality necessary to stardom appears here: in not giving all she can, Emmagene is trying to avoid vulnerability. But a star mustn't be
invulnerable. As Tallulah tells Jeanmarie, "An unscarred performer is truly empty calories: sweet but not nourishing" (*U*,
157).

Jeanmarie accepts this dictum and takes risks: she reads a
poem to an audience and tries out for a part in the school play.
In taking the risks, she triumphs. Malcolm, too, has learned how
to be a star. He learns along with Jeanmarie that one must embody the four qualities discussed above, and more: he learns
that one must also cultivate balance. Tallulah has told him a
balance between feeling and thinking is necessary to performer
or to scientist. The idea of balance, in fact, is a major theme of
Tel.

Of course, the book demonstrates the principle of balance in
its two main characters. Thus Jeanmarie composes the weathergrams but can't beautifully inscribe them; Malcolm, the tidily
self-controlled one, can. Further, only Malcolm can use the IRS
computer to find two of the three buskers, but Jeanmarie identifies Emmagene at Washington Square through intuition. Jeanmarie partially succeeds through intuition; she wholly succeeds
in her quest for "stardom," though, thanks to Malcolm and his
logical approach. Malcolm, the thinker, does not just complete
Jeanmarie, however. Growing in his own right, he comes to
realize there is more to life than facts. Once he realizes that fact,
he can intuit why Emmagene failed. He, too, we sense, finds
"balance." He has grown beyond the merely rational sixth-
grader of the book's opening chapters.

This theme of balance appears crystallized in one of Tallulah's epigraphs toward the close of the book: *"If ever you want to
learn the difference between accuracy and truth, look at a photograph of Gertrude Stein and then look at Picasso's portrait of
her"* (*U*, 166). As Malcolm learns, "accuracy" is not enough—not
enough for the scientist, not enough for any seeker after truth
on the "star" level. The word *star* has a broader meaning than

that which Jeanmarie implies as she introduces the concept early in the book. "Star" is a metaphor for success; we need not be very perceptive to realize that Jeanmarie's success in the (sixth-grade) theater is part of a larger theme that explores how to approach any dream. Talent, timing, generosity, the willingness to be vulnerable: these qualities ensure success beyond the stage. One cannot easily think of any dream, any task, that cannot be accomplished if a child (or an adult) combines those four qualities in its pursuit.

Conclusion

In *Journey to an 800 Number* and *Up from Jericho Tel* Konigsburg again explores a child's need for other children (and for adults, if the ghostly Tallulah counts as an adult). As in *Jennifer*, Konigsburg begins both books with children who are loners; both Bo and Jeanmarie find not only an adult guide, but someone close to their own age with whom to make an "us" during the course of their books. And again, as always for Konigsburg, the children discover or construct major elements of their identities at the same time.

Afterword

E. L. Konigsburg's books are short. The longest, *A Proud Taste for Scarlet and Miniver*, has 201 pages; the shortest, *Altogether, One at a Time*, has 79. Thus the first reading of each book goes quickly (I say "first" because, as librarians and parents attest, children reread these books). Children may reread Konigsburg's books for several reasons: the chief reason, though, reflects the quality dear to the Renaissance—and one Konigsburg discusses in an essay—that of *sprezzatura*. In *The Book of the Courtier* (*Il libro de cortegiano* [ca. 1512]) Baldesar Castiglione says that "we may affirm that to be true art which does not appear to be art,"[1] or, as Konigsburg puts it, "Works of art must have weight and knowing beneath them.... [W]orks of art must have all the techniques and all the skills; they must never be sloppy but never show the gears. Make it nonchalant, easy, light" (*"Sprezzatura,"* 261).

That nonchalance, or lightness, is *sprezzatura*, and it is Konigsburg's chief strength. It is true that her plots—each unique—possess a compelling element of the "What next?" and that her characters are likable and able to be identified with, often pleasingly subversive of adult values. But children reread her for her *sprezzatura* in style and theme.

If works embodying *sprezzatura* "must have weight and knowing beneath them," there is no weightier issue in children's literature than Konigsburg's theme of identity. To be sure, sexuality and divorce and sibling relationships and filial relationships and coping with single-parent families and coping with blended families are important, even essential, themes for contemporary children's literature. A child can successfully cope with none of these issues, however, unless she/he first finds someplace to stand. Firm footing in one's own identity, of course, does not automatically solve problems arising from these other

163

issues, but identity must come first if the child is to resolve the remainder.

Of course Konigsburg is not alone in her possessing a unique, witty style and profound theme. Throughout this study I have compared her books with those of such other excellent children's writers as Bruce Brooks, Betsy Byars, Eleanor Cameron, Vera and Bill Cleaver, Brock Cole, Barbara Corcoran, Marguerite de Angeli, Louise Fitzhugh, Jean George, Virginia Hamilton, Janni Howker, Katherine Paterson, Ouida Sebestyen, and Cynthia Voigt, many of whom, like Konigsburg, have received the Newbery Award and/or the Newbery Honor Book Award for their books' stylistic excellence and thematic significance.

As one might expect, each of these comparable writers (and many other fine writers I hadn't the space to discuss) differs in style from the others. All are alike, though, and similar to Konigsburg, in their choice of theme: their protagonists grow—explore their identities—during the stories. These writers' works are also alike in that each ends on a hopeful note; none ends with the distinctly pessimistic tone of books like Robert Cormier's *The Chocolate War* (1974).

What makes Konigsburg different from other upbeat authors is, first, the uniqueness of her plots, which are unique to her in a way that the plots of other fine books are sometimes not so to their authors. All Voigt's books, for example, have a similar plot line: members of a family are somehow separated from someone—usually another family member, sometimes a significant other—with whom they seek to be united. With Konigsburg, in contrast, no two plots have been even roughly similar.

Second, and of chief importance, it is Konigsburg's consistently witty style that most distinguishes her. No children's writer I have read is as consistently witty as Elaine Lobl Konigsburg. More than any other children's author, she writes easily and lightly, though with weight and knowing underneath. Her books may not work for all 8- to 12-year-olds, but they do work for the brightest readers of any age.

Konigsburg published her first picture book in 1990; her second was published in 1991, and her third was in press in 1992. The first, *Samuel Todd's Book of Great Colors,* shows a new direction for Konigsburg as she expands the techniques and skills she used for years as she illustrated her own books. Design is pre-eminent in *Colors,* with color a major element; the text, though still "nonchalant, easy, light," is tertiary. Thus one entire page holds only "Blueberries and blue jays are blue, and they is why they aren't called yellowberries and orange jays" (19). The understated wit will appeal to the book's audience, but those 17 words are almost 20 percent of the total text of 311 words.

The picture books mark a new direction; whether Konigsburg will return to children's novels remains to be seen. In any event, her 12 longer books as of 1992 will doubtless remain in print. She has fulfilled the promise signaled by the simultaneous winning of the Newbery Award and the Newbery Honor Book Award for her first two books.

Notes and References

Preface

1. Both books appeared in 1967 owing to Konigsburg's editor, Jean Karl. Karl read *Jennifer, Hecate, Macbeth, William McKinley, and Me, Elizabeth* in 1967, thought it excellent, and scheduled it for publication in 1967. Karl read *From the Mixed-up Files of Mrs. Basil E. Frankweiler* in 1967, thought it too good to hold back, and scheduled it for rush publication. Jean Karl, "Elaine L. Konigsburg," in *Authors and Illustrators of Children's Books: Writings on Their Lives and Works*, ed. Miriam Hoffman and Eva Samuels (New York and London: Bowker, 1972), 244–45.

2. Eric A. Kimmel, "Jewish Identity in Juvenile Fiction: A Look at Three Recommended Books," *Horn Book*, April 1973; reprinted in *Crosscurrents of Criticism: Horn Book Essays 1968–1977*, ed. Paul Heins (Boston: Horn Book, 1977), 150–58; hereafter cited in text. David Rees, "Your Arcane Novelist—E. L. Konigsburg: An English Viewpoint," *Horn Book* 54 (1978): 79–85; hereafter cited in text. John Rowe Townsend, "E. L. Konigsburg," in *A Sounding of Storytellers* (New York: Lippincott, 1979), 111–24; hereafter cited in text.

3. *Files* had gone through 27 printings as of 1990 (interview with Konigsburg, 29 June 1990; hereafter cited in text).

4. "Newbery Award Acceptance," *Horn Book* 44 (1968): 392–95; hereafter cited in text as "NAA."

5. "Profile: Elaine Konigsburg," interview with Linda T. Jones, *Language Arts* 63 (1986): 179; hereafter cited in text as "Jones interview."

6. Erik Erikson, *Identity: Youth and Crisis* (New York: Norton, 1968), 91–96, 128–35; hereafter cited in text.

1. Biographical Sketch

1. Reported by Konigsburg in an interview published in *Contemporary Authors*, vol. 17 (New Revision Series), ed. Linda Metzger and Deborah A. Straub (Detroit: Gale Research Co., 1986), 251; hereafter cited in text as "*CA* interview."

2. Interview with Konigsburg, 6 January 1989; hereafter cited in text.

3. Thus not only does chemistry figure prominently in her 1970 novel—*(George)*—but also she was commissioned to write the retrospective essay on 1983 Nobel Prize winner Barbara McClintock for the *Nobel Prize Annual: 1988* (New York: I. M. G. Publishing, 1989), 14.

4. She has also written a series of published and unpublished essays and speeches about writing children's books, and the *Nobel Prize Annual* "retrospective" on Barbara McClintock.

5. For example, in "Ruthie Britten and Because I Can," in *Celebrating Children's Books: Essays . . . in Honor of Zena Sutherland*, ed. Betsy Hearne and Marilyn Kaye (New York: Lothrop, Lee, and Shepard, 1981), 71.

2. Moving Inside the Outsiders

1. *Jennifer, Hecate, Macbeth, William McKinley, and Me, Elizabeth* (New York: Atheneum, 1967), 4; hereafter cited in text as *J*.

2. Jennifer's race was not at first apparent to me when I read the book. Several readers have told me they did not realize Jennifer was black until Elizabeth reports of the PTA audience, "I saw Jennifer's mother. . . . I knew it was Jennifer's mother because she was the only Black mother there" (*J*, 56). The drawings are, to my eye, ambiguous; once we know Jennifer is black, she looks black to us in the illustrations. Konigsburg told me in January 1989 that she had not intentionally made her illustrations ambiguous. I think the ambiguity fortunate.

3. David Rees suggests the restrictive element in the relationship is not the supposed witchcraft but "the point that friendship is limited, frustrating even, when one of the two people is domineering and the other meekly subservient" (Rees, 82–83).

4. John Rowe Townsend stimulated my thinking on this theme in his paragraph on the white-black relationship in *Jennifer*. He suggests that Jennifer's being black is both subtle and essential, and adds that "by force of character she has made something positive from being the odd one out" (Townsend, 114).

5. Nancy Larrick, "The All-White World of Children's Books," *Saturday Review*, 11 September 1965.

6. Noted by Konigsburg in "*Sprezzatura*: A Kind of Excellence," *Horn Book* 52 (1976): 254; hereafter cited in text as "*Sprezzatura*."

7. She and her family had waited a long, cold time in line outside the Metropolitan Museum of Art to see the Mona Lisa in the winter of 1963, then were not impressed ("*Sprezzatura*," 254).

8. Konigsburg's account, quoted from Townsend, 123–24.

9. *From the Mixed-up Files of Mrs. Basil E. Frankweiler* (New York: Atheneum, 1967), 38; hereafter cited in text as *F*.

10. This passage qualifies as indecent to some readers. See Konigsburg's "Excerpts from My Bouboulina File," *Library Quarterly* 51 (1981): 68–79.

11. Townsend also suggests, however, that using the Frankweiler narrator allows "some adult insights" and adds the "pleasing subtlety" of a "bond between the generations" that forms between Claudia and Mrs. Frankweiler (Townsend, 116).

12. George, like Konigsburg, illustrates her own book.

3. Moving Inward

1. *About the B'nai Bagels* (New York: Atheneum, 1969); hereafter cited in text as *BB*.

2. Bessie's lack of orthodoxy, not only in praying but in most of her religious observances, troubles Eric A. Kimmel. He deplores Konigsburg's approach to Jewish life, complaining that the Setzers "function as Jews" merely by blindly following a few customs (e.g., avoiding leavened bread on Passover). "From the Jewish point of view," he concludes, "they represent a dying Jewishness" (Kimmel, 158). These are harsh words. Kimmel may perhaps be charged with asking of the book something it does not intend to provide. Konigsburg has written of a modern American boy finding his identity. His finding it—his "becoming," as he puts it—happens to take place in the context of a suburban Jewish family. Konigsburg simply has not focused on Kimmel's preferred issue, "modern American Jewish life" (Kimmel, 158). To judge her book as if she had tried to write on that topic but failed is to misjudge it.

3. Bessie's character is so enjoyable, and so central to Mark's development, that John Rowe Townsend found *Bagels* essentially her book (Townsend, 118). He concludes that the book is "attractive and funny, though not very important" (118). Bessie Setzer is certainly important in the book. In the final analysis, though, most readers will find *Bagels* Mark Setzer's book, not his mother's. Those same readers may feel that Mark's particular path to identity is, though not earth-shaking, at least important.

4. Bruce Brooks, *The Moves Make the Man* (New York: Harper & Row, 1984), 256.

5. *(George)* (New York: Atheneum, 1970), 3; hereafter cited in text as *G*.

6. *Forms of Intellectual and Ethical Development in the College Years: A Scheme* (New York: Holt, Rinehart & Winston, 1970). Swarms of studies since Perry's pioneering work have substantiated and/or re-

fined his observations; a review of these studies, and of Perry's, appears in Joanne G. Kurfiss, "Developmental Foundations of Critical Thinking," *Critical Thinking: Theory, Research, Practice, and Possibilities*, ASHE-ERIC Higher Education Report No. 2 (Washington, D.C.: Association for the Study of Higher Education, 1988), 51–70.

7. As in *Children and Books*, 6th ed., ed. Zena Sutherland et al. (Glenview, Ill.: Scott, Foresman, 1981), 327.

8. Betsy Byars, *The Summer of the Swans* (New York: Viking, 1970), 37, 121.

4. The Short Stories

1. *Altogether, One at a Time* (New York: Atheneum, 1971), 4; hereafter cited in the text as *A*.

2. Cynthia Voigt, *Homecoming* (New York: Atheneum, 1981), 295.

3. As I pointed out earlier, this is Konigsburg's sole autobiographical story. Much of it happened to her when she was a nine-year-old in Youngstown, Ohio.

4. Note that the book appeared in 1971, five years before Alex Haley's *Roots* was published and became a national best-seller.

5. "Of Ariel, Caliban, and Certain Beasts of Mine Own," *Proceedings of the Seventh Annual Conference of The Children's Literature Association, Baylor University, March 1980*, ed. Priscilla Ord (New Rochelle, N.Y.: Children's Literature Association, 1982), 6.

6. *Throwing Shadows* (New York: Atheneum, 1979), 3; hereafter cited in the text as *T*.

5. The Historical Novels

1. *A Proud Taste for Scarlet and Miniver* (New York: Atheneum, 1973), 4; hereafter cited in text as *PT*.

2. Amy Kelly, *Eleanor of Aquitaine and the Four Kings* (Cambridge, Mass.: Harvard University Press, 1950), 49.

3. Kelly's *Eleanor of Aquitaine and the Four Kings* is still the standard biography (see p. 100 for "The Matter of Britain").

4. *The Horizon Book of the Renaissance* (New York: American Heritage Publishing Co., 1961), 185–92.

5. *The Second Mrs. Giaconda* (New York: Atheneum, 1975), 3; hereafter cited in text as *S*.

6. History suggests that da Vinci and Salai had a homosexual relationship (Kenneth Clark, *Leonardo da Vinci: An Account of His Development as an Artist* [Harmondsworth, England: Penguin, 1967], 58; herafter cited in text). Konigsburg writes that she excluded that rela-

tionship from a book for children, both because she thought it unsuitable (or so she implies) and because she thought a solely sexual relationship insufficient to explain their "twenty- or . . . twenty-five-year relationship" ("*Sprezzatura*," 258).

7. For a look at "the subversive" in children's literature see Alison Lurie's *Don't Tell the Grown-ups: Subversive Children's Literature* (Boston: Little, Brown, 1990).

8. This theme of "wildness" first appeared in *(George)*, in an early passage characterizing George's approach to problems: "Sometimes it would be a zany word . . . or sometimes just a *wild* point of view" (*G,* 9; my italics).

9. Elizabeth Ripley, *Leonardo da Vinci* (Oxford: Oxford University Press, 1952), 30.

10. John Rowe Townsend finds "bright surfaces but a . . . lack of emotional depth" in the two historical novels (Townsend, 121). He nonetheless considers *Proud Taste* "as good in its way" (122) as her Newbery Award winners. David Rees is unimpressed, suggesting that that "the stories [of both] are not sufficiently exciting in themselves," whereas in her other works one wants to keep turning pages to find out what happens (Rees, 84).

6. Freeing the Imprisoned

1. *The Dragon in the Ghetto Caper* (New York: Atheneum, 1974), 9; hereafter cited in text as *D.*

2. See Margaret Freeman's *The Unicorn Tapestries* (New York: Metropolitan Museum of Art [Dutton], 1976) for color reproductions and explications of the tapestries.

3. David Rees does not discuss *Dragon*; John Rowe Townsend dismisses the book's dragons as "portentously symbolic," the plot as "neither convincing nor particularly interesting" (Townsend, 120).

4. *Father's Arcane Daughter* (New York: Atheneum, 1976), 118; hereafter cited in text as *F.*

7. Finding Yourself—and Someone Else

1. *Journey to an 800 Number* (New York: Atheneum, 1982), 121; hereafter cited in text as *J.*

2. *Up from Jericho Tel* (New York: Atheneum, 1986), 15; hereafter cited in text as *U.*

3. This and the other animal burials in *Tel* remind one of the plot of the 1952 movie *Forbidden Games* described in chapter 10 of *Father's Arcane Daughter*. In it Michel and his friend Paulette bury Paulette's dead dog, "a mole, and other small dead animals they find" (*F,* 90). The

burials somehow bring the friendship of Michel and Paulette to a focus, as they do the friendship of Jeanmarie and Malcolm in *Tel*.

4. Adult readers will recognize Tallulah Bankhead. Child readers probably will not, but Konigsburg's descriptions and characterization satisfactorily identify "Tallulah" as a stage and screen star without the background an adult carries to the book.

5. Malcolm repeatedly tells the ghostly Tallulah she shouldn't smoke, to which she once returns, "Don't worry, darling, it won't kill me" (*U*, 27).

6. Konigsburg has said that "in the higher reaches . . . science and art are one" ("*CA* interview," 251), a suggestion that takes on fictive life in *Tel*'s Malcolm.

Afterword

1. In *World Masterpieces*, trans. Leonard E. Opdycke, 3d ed., vol. 1, ed. Maynard Mack et al. (New York: Norton, 1973), 1234.

Selected Bibliography

Primary Works

Novels

About the B'nai Bagels. New York: Atheneum, 1969.

The Dragon in the Ghetto Caper. New York: Atheneum, 1974.

Father's Arcane Daughter. New York: Atheneum, 1976.

From the Mixed-up Files of Mrs. Basil E. Frankweiler. New York: Atheneum, 1967.

(George). New York: Atheneum, 1970.

Jennifer, Hecate, Macbeth, William McKinley, and Me, Elizabeth. New York: Atheneum, 1967.

Journey to an 800 Number. New York: Atheneum, 1982.

A Proud Taste for Scarlet and Miniver. New York: Atheneum, 1973.

The Second Mrs. Giaconda. New York: Atheneum, 1975.

Up from Jericho Tel. New York: Atheneum, 1986.

Short Stories

Altogether, One at a Time. New York: Atheneum, 1971.

Throwing Shadows. New York: Atheneum, 1979.

Picture Books

Amy Elizabeth Explores Bloomingdale's. New York: Atheneum, 1992.

Samuel Todd's Book of Great Colors. New York: Atheneum, 1990.

Samuel Todd's Book of Great Inventions. New York: Atheneum, 1991.

Essays

"Barbara McClintock: Retrospective." *Nobel Prize Annual: 1988.* New York: I. M. G. Publishing, 1989. An overview of McClintock's career and an examination of her manner of working.

"The Double Image: Language as the Perimeter of Culture." *School Li-*

brary Journal 17 (February 1970): 31–34. A survey of suburban language as compared to the ceremonial bragging of the Kwakiutl Indians, and a suggestion that language sets the perimeters of a child's thinking.

"Excerpts from My Bouboulina File." *Library Quarterly* 51 (1981): 68–79. Discusses censorship of the standing-on-the-toilet segment of *Files* and other instances of censorship.

"Newbery Award Acceptance." *Horn Book* 44 (1968): 391–95. Establishes Konigsburg's interest in writing about the suburbs and about children's identities.

"Of Ariel, Caliban, and Certain Beasts of Mine Own." *Proceedings of the Seventh Annual Conference of the Children's Literature Association, Baylor University, March 1980,* edited by Priscilla Ord. New Rochelle, N.Y.: Children's Literature Association, 1982. Discusses a child's discovering the monster inside him/herself and overcoming the monster with decency.

"Ruthie Britten and Because I Can." *Celebrating Children's Books: Essays ... in Honor of Zena Sutherland,* edited by Betsy Hearne and Marilyn Kaye. New York: Lothrop, Lee & Shepard, 1981. Contains an explanation of why Konigsburg writes for children.

"*Sprezzatura:* A Kind of Excellence." *Horn Book* 52 (1976): 253–61. Discusses the genesis of *The Second Mrs. Giaconda* and explains the concept of *sprezzatura.*

Secondary Works

Hanks, D. Thomas, Jr. "The Wit of E. L. Konigsburg." *Studies in American Humor* 5, no. 4 (1986–87; published 1990): 243–54. Discusses wit and humor in Konigsburg's works.

Jones, Linda T. "Profile: Elaine Konigsburg." Interview. *Language Arts* 63 (1986): 177–84. Contains a full discussion of Konigsburg's writing practices and her statement that her one theme is "identity."

Karl, Jean. "Elaine L. Konigsburg." In *Authors and Illustrators of Children's Books: Writings on Their Lives and Works,* edited by Miriam Hoffman and Eva Samuels. New York and London: Bowker, 1972. Contains the background of the publication of *Jennifer* and *Files.*

Kimmel, Eric A. "Jewish Identity in Juvenile Fiction: A Look at Three Recommended Books." *Horn Book,* April 1973. Reprinted in *Crosscurrents of Criticism: Horn Book Essays, 1968–1977,* edited by Paul Heins. Boston: Horn Book, 1977. One of the three "recommended books" is *Bagels,* which Kimmel deplores as a superficial treatment of Judaism.

"Konigsburg, E[laine] L[obl]. 1930–." In *Contemporary Authors*, edited by Linda Metzger and Deborah A. Straub. Vol. 17 (New Revision Series). Detroit: Gale Research, 1986. Contains full listings of works and awards as of 1985, a comprehensive biography, and a telephone interview with Konigsburg.

Rees, David. "Your Arcane Novelist—E. L. Konigsburg: An English Viewpoint." *Horn Book* 54 (1978): 79–85. Critically assesses Konigsburg's works through *Father's Arcane Daughter* (1976), discussing especially style and the theme of identity.

Townsend, John Rowe. "E. L. Konigsburg." In *A Sounding of Storytellers*. New York: Lippincott, 1979. Discusses Konigsburg's work through *The Second Mrs. Giaconda* (1975).

Index

The Author

Dorrel T. Hanks, Jr., is professor of English at Baylor University, Waco, Texas, where he teaches writing, medieval English literature, and children's literature. He received his B.A. and M.A. in English from Washington University and his Ph.D. in medieval English literature from the University of Minnesota. His essays have appeared in *Children's Literature;* the *Children's Literature Association Quarterly;* the *Journal of Popular Culture; Studies in American Humor; Popular Culture in the Middle Ages,* edited by Josie P. Campbell (1986); and *The Figure of Merlin in the Nineteenth and Twentieth Centuries,* edited by Jeanie Watson and Maureen Fries (1989).

The Editor

Ruth K. MacDonald is a professor of English and head of the Department of English and Philosophy at Purdue University. She received her B.A. and M.A. in English from the University of Connecticut, her Ph.D. in English from Rutgers University, and her M.B.A. from the University of Texas at El Paso. To Twayne's United States and English Authors series she has contributed the volumes on Louisa May Alcott, Beatrix Potter, and Dr. Seuss. She is the author of *Literature for Children in England and America, 1646–1774* (1982).